D1556971

Icelandic Poems and Stories

ICELANDIC POEMS AND STORIES

Translations from Modern Icelandic Literature

EDITED BY RICHARD BECK

Granger Index Reprint Series

Originally published by:
PRINCETON UNIVERSITY PRESS
FOR THE AMERICAN-SCANDINAVIAN FOUNDATION

BOOKS FOR LIBRARIES PRESS
FREEPORT, NEW YORK

Reprinted from a copy in the collections of
The New York Public Library
Astor, Lenox and Tilden Foundations

LIBRARY OF CONGRESS CATALOG CARD NUMBER:
68-57059

CONTENTS

Icelandic Poems and Stories

INTRODUCTION

THE last hundred years have been a remarkable period in the history of Icelandic literature, no less than in the political and cultural history of the Icelandic people. The national awakening, which found expression in an ever growing demand for the restoration of Icelandic independence as well as in many-sided material progress, was further manifested during this period by a vigorous expansion of the national spirit and genius in varied literary and artistic activity.

Poetry, the time-honored form of literary expression among the Icelanders, has flourished as never before since the days of the ancient skalds. This is true particularly of the first half of the period, not to minimize the prominent part which the lyric poets are playing in the literary and cultural life of present-day Iceland. Comparatively speaking, their number is still very large, although prose writers now rival them and in some degree may be said to overshadow them in the attention of the Icelandic reading public. In not a few cases, however, as will become clear in the course of this introductory account of Icelandic literature, lyric poets have also written prose of equal, not to say greater, significance.

I

TWO main currents vitalize the Icelandic poetry of the earlier half of the period under consideration: on the one hand, influences from abroad, notably the Romantic Movement; on the other, a renewed and strengthened interest in the native Icelandic literary heritage and tradition, which had never lost its hold upon the poets and prose writers of Iceland down through the intervening centuries. Moreover, it was only natural that the Romantic Movement, with its nationalism and its strong and idealistic interest in the past, should turn the eyes of Icelandic poets to the history of their nation and lead to renewed study of its rich ancient literature, which, in turn, with its classic restraint, saved them, virtually without exception, from the aberrations and excesses of many Romantic poets elsewhere.

This is clearly seen in the poems of the man who introduced Romanticism into Icelandic literature, Bjarni Thorarensen, in whom the foreign influence of the Romantic Movement, particularly of Oehlenschläger, is easily traceable side by side with an even stronger and deeper current deriving from older Icelandic literature. The same is true, although in a somewhat different sense, of Thorarensen's younger contemporary, Jónas Hallgrímsson, in whose poetry the characteristic Romantic love of beauty and of nature find exquisite and delicate expression.

The native Icelandic tradition is especially strong in the works of Sigurdur Breidfjörd, the chief master of the so-called *rímur*-poetry, alliterative and narrative ballads extremely popular in Iceland from ancient times almost to the turn of the century; and in the more vigorous and original poems of Hjálmar Jónsson (Bólu-Hjálmar) whose rugged poetic genius rose above the humblest and most adverse circumstances. To these gifted unschooled poets of the peasant class, although he might properly be called a "gentleman-farmer," belonged also Páll Ólafsson, whose mature work falls, however, within the latter half of the century.

During that era a whole array of uncommonly gifted poets, such as Grímur Thomsen, Benedikt Gröndal, Steingrímur Thorsteinsson, Matthías Jochumsson, and Kristján Jónsson, carried on the Romantic tradition of Thorarensen and Hallgrímsson. As in the work of these pioneer Romanticists of Iceland, there is in the poetry of their successors a national undercurrent, which in a great many cases is stronger than the foreign trend. In fact, very often these poets find both inspiration and subject-matter in the sagas and the history of their nation. The hold of the native tradition upon them is further seen in the use of ancient Icelandic verse-forms which is no uncommon practice on the part of their present-day successors. All this goes to prove the unbroken continuity of the Icelandic literary tradition, an appreciation of which is necessary to the true understanding of the history of Icelandic letters as a whole.

The course of the Realistic Movement in Icelandic literature further emphasizes the vigor of the native tradition. Traces of Brandesian Realism may be found in the early writings of Jón Ólafsson, a radical patriot and poet, who translated some of the works of Kristofer Janson and Björnstjerne Björnson into Icelandic. The chief representatives of the Realistic Movement in Icelandic letters were, however, Gestur Pálsson and Einar Hjörleifsson Kvaran, noted particularly as writers of short stories and novels, and the lyric poet Hannes Hafstein. They belonged to a group of four Icelandic students in Copenhagen, who, under the influence of Georg Brandes, founded the periodical *Ver-*

dandi in 1882 for the avowed purpose of championing Realism in the literature of their homeland. Although only one volume appeared, the publication is of importance as it aroused much discussion in Icelandic literary circles and was the harbinger of new and challenging ideas. Nevertheless, it did not bring about any sharp or lasting cleavage in Icelandic literature, which has always been rooted in the realities of life, showing in many ways its closeness to the soil. The native literary tradition more than held its own. This is strikingly illustrated in the work of Thorsteinn Erlingsson, one of the most influential poets of the period. During his student days in Copenhagen he had also come under the influence of Brandes and his followers, although he was not a member of the *Verdandi* group. Uncommonly militant in his socialist and rationalist views, he was none the less profoundly faithful to the Icelandic literary tradition, and excelled in the old *rímur*-meter, paying tribute to the older masters in that realm, such as Sigurdur Breidfjörd.

Of the long list of gifted Icelandic poets whose maturer years belong to the earlier part of the present century, the following are among the most significant: Sigurjón Fridjónsson, Thorsteinn Gíslason, Gudmundur Gudmundsson, and Sigurdur Sigurdsson. All of them have written lyric poetry of a high order, especially the last named, whose best efforts possess rare poetic beauty. The twin peaks among Icelandic poets of that generation are, however, Einar Benediktsson and Stephan G. Stephansson, both of whom unquestionably rank with the greatest Icelandic poets of all time, by virtue of their high imaginative quality, robust intellect, and superb mastery of their native tongue. Because of the central place which Stephansson thus occupies in the history of Icelandic literature, he is the only one of a considerable group of notable Icelandic poets in America to be included in this volume.

Present-day Icelandic poetry has in a high degree the pattern of an entrancing mosaic. The works of the leading poets reflect numerous tendencies and are therefore not readily classified. While the Realistic approach to life is characteristic of some, others are of a more Romantic or Neo-Romantic bent of mind. Generally speaking, the national note is nevertheless still very strong, with a pronounced interest in folk-poetry and folklore. At the same time Icelandic poetry has in recent years been enriched both by new themes and no less by a greater variety of verse forms. Stefán Sigurdsson (frá Hvítadal), whose lyric vein at its best was of the purest kind, introduced many exquisite and much imitated meters, in some cases with Ibsen, Per Sivle, and other Norwegian writers as his models.

His most important immediate contemporaries, whose mature production belongs to the last quarter century, are Örn Arnarson (Magnús Stefánsson) who succeeds admirably in harmonizing thought and form; Jakob Thorarensen, whose descriptive poems are notable alike for their vigor and vividness; and Jakob Jóhannesson Smári, the Icelandic master of the sonnet.

Unnur Benediktsdóttir (Hulda) is one of several women poets of the older generation, including Theodora Thoroddsen, who have made a significant contribution to modern Icelandic literature in verse and prose. Not a few of their younger sisters are emulating their example in a most worthy fashion.

Davíd Stefánsson (frá Fagraskógi) is a gifted and popular representative of a large group of younger men poets, who carry on brilliantly the best tradition of Icelandic lyric poetry. Only the most outstanding of his contemporaries can be enumerated here. Jón Magnússon recently published the most important epic poem of the day, *Björn á Reydarfelli,* a lasting monument to many of the finest qualities in the Icelandic national character. Jóhannes Jónasson (Jóhannes úr Kötlum) is the author of excellently wrought patriotic poems and challenging social satires. Tómas Gudmundsson, a master craftsman, has a place of his own for his original and whimsical portrayal of the life and the local characteristics of Reykjavík, the capital of Iceland. Magnús Ásgeirsson is the master-translator among Icelandic poets of today, while Gudmundur Bödvarsson, a young farmer, is noted for his well-wrought, strongly personal poems and nature descriptions, which are rich with still greater promise of things to come.

II

THE novel in the modern sense of the word is indeed a very recent phase of Icelandic literature, but the narrative art as such is nearly as ancient a form of literary expression among the Icelanders as is the art of poetry. The Icelandic sagas, with their quick turns of dialogue, excellent plot construction, and vivid characterization, anticipated in many respects the modern novel. Writing stories in prose was therefore nothing new to the Icelander of the last century; he was carrying on, in a somewhat different form to be sure, a cherished literary tradition of his race; grafting, as it were, a new branch on an ancient tree.

Jónas Hallgrímsson was the first to attempt writing modern Icelandic fiction, the most noteworthy result being his charming little story *Grasaferdin* (Gathering Icelandic Moss), a romantic idyl describing rural life in Iceland. He may, therefore, with some justification, be looked upon as the father of modern Icelandic fiction, although it is a far cry from his simple tale to the present-day short story.

It was Jón Thoroddsen, however, who became the pioneer novelist of Iceland with his novels *Piltur og stúlka* (Lad and Lass, 1850) and *Madur og kona* (Man and Wife, 1876), which present vivid and truthful pictures of contemporary rural life in Iceland. The first of these, a veritable landmark in the literary history of Iceland, presents two characters who have long since become proverbial types in Iceland, and contains the ever popular patriotic song, "Ó, fögur er vor fósturjörd" (O lovely is our fatherland), a delightful description of Iceland in its summer and winter garb. His second novel, although unfortunately incomplete, further reveals his narrative skill and even more so his mastery of characterization, especially in picturing comic or otherwise striking individuals. It has been established that many of these were drawn directly from real life. While Thoroddsen thus wisely harvested his themes in the everyday life about him in Iceland, and drew heavily on Icelandic folklore, he also found inspiration in some of the novels of Sir Walter Scott dealing with country life. His concise and robust style, racy and Icelandic to the core, lends attraction to his literary work, as does also the spontaneous humor that invests his stories with life and color.

Several of Thoroddsen's contemporaries tried their hand at writing fiction, more or less in the Romantic vein, but on the whole with only indifferent success. It therefore remained for the Realists to lift the short story and the novel to a new level of literary excellence and social significance. This was achieved by such leading writers of that group as Gestur Pálsson, Einar Hjörleifsson Kvaran, and Jón Stefánsson (Thorgils Gjallandi), together with their younger contemporaries Gudmundur Fridjónsson and Gudmundur Magnússon (Jón Trausti), both of whom produced some of the finest short stories in the Icelandic language. The latter also described life in Iceland, past and present, in several memorable novels, told with the skill of a born story-teller and a keen observer of human nature.

Icelandic fiction, no less than the poetry of the last quarter century, the period following the First World War, presents a motley picture of conflicting forms, a constant interplay of the old and the new. Romanticism, Neo-Romanticism, and Realism have their adherents, while social satire in the spirit of Socialism and Communism have even more ardent devotees, especially among the younger group. Any individual classification of these writers would lead too far afield. Limitation of space excludes mention of all but the most important.

Kristín Sigfúsdóttir has made a name for herself with her novels and short stories of country life. She is, however, far surpassed in productivity and literary significance by Gudmundur Gíslason Hagalín and Halldór Kiljan Laxness, two authors who, though widely different, have both gained a secure place among the prose writers of Iceland, as interpreters of various phases of national life and as masters of a rich, highly individual style. Davíd Stefánsson was for years the most popular lyric poet of the day; with his first full-length novel and a no less remarkable drama, both profoundly national in theme, he has grown in stature as an author and taken his place with the masters of Icelandic prose.

Another novelist who has come to the forefront in Iceland during the last few years is Elinborg Lárusdóttir. She has written good short stories, but her major work to date is her three-volume novel *Förumann* (Vagrants), presenting a crowded canvas of widely different characters. This significant novel, which is somewhat uneven in excellence, as is only to be expected in a work of such magnitude, is an important historical-social document, for the author has made a thorough study of the background and factual material which is the warp and woof of her narrative. Thórir Bergsson (Thorsteinn Jónsson), a bank clerk, has also written a first novel on Icelandic rural life, characterized by penetration, truthfulness, and a polished, fluent style; but these qualities are seen to still greater advantage in his excellently wrought short stories, which mark him as one of the finest Icelandic craftsmen in that difficult field of concentrated fiction.

Sigurdur Nordal, who is a rare combination of the erudite scholar and the highly imaginative poet, has written some masterly short stories, but has made a still more important contribution to modern Icelandic literature with his admirably constructed prose-poems, fraught with ideas expressed in a sparkling lyric style, which struck a definitely new note. He also occupies a central position as a literary critic and essayist. The same is true, although in a different sense, of Thórbergur Thórdarson, a radical of radicals in his literary no less than in his social views. His mastery of the most varied types of Icelandic style is a fundamental characteristic of his essays on numerous divergent subjects and of his autobiographical writings, often mercilessly satirical. Undeniably an eccentric by temperament, whose predilection for bitter satire of social and literary convention has made him the center of numerous controversies, Thórdarson has, however, been a potent factor in present-day Icelandic literature, and his influence is clearly seen in the style of such leading writers as Hagalín and Laxness, to mention only two of the best known.

In a large group of younger prose writers, several of whom show considerable promise, Gudmundur Daníelsson (frá Guttormshaga) merits special mention. A public school teacher by profession, he has already written several novels on contemporary life in Iceland, social and critical in mood, but showing a steadily growing mastery of subject matter, style, and characterization. That is particularly clear from his latest novel, *Af jörd ertu kominn* (Dust Thou art), the first volume of a work of large dimensions and much more than ordinary penetration.

The important group of Icelandic authors who have made Danish or Norwegian their principal literary medium includes, besides the dramatist Jóhann Sigurjónsson and the novelist Kristmann Gudmundsson, two others of the most gifted and most widely famed Icelandic writers of our day, Gunnar Gunnarsson and Gudmundur Kamban.

Gunnarsson, who is represented in the volume *Denmark's Best Stories* in this series, stands in the front rank among the world's novelists today. He has written nearly all his works in the Danish language, though usually with an Icelandic background, and it is indicative of his strong attachment to his native land, that, at the height of his international fame, he has returned to Iceland and has bought a farm in the eastern part of the country, where he spent his childhood and where his forebears had lived for generations. Gunnarsson has been enormously productive. Several of his important books, including the three first volumes, *Ships in the Sky* (two volumes in one) and *The Night and the Dream*, of his monumental series of autobiographical novels, are available in English translation. Here his profound insight, his unusual ability to reveal the innermost soul-life of his characters, is evident together with his brilliant technical skill.

Kamban, a leading dramatist no less than a novelist, whose works have appeared in both Icelandic and Danish, has likewise been a very productive author. With some of his plays he has achieved stage successes in the Scandinavian countries. His most significant achievement in the realm of fiction is his historical novel *Skálholt*, a broad dramatic recreation of seventeenth century Iceland, in which a large number of memorable characters are portrayed against a vividly drawn, colorful background. The first two parts of this notable work have appeared in an English translation under the title *The Virgin of Skalholt*.

Brief as the above survey of necessity is, it gives none the less some idea of the richness and variety of modern Icelandic literature, selected examples of which, in verse and prose, are found on the following pages. As is always the case with the literature of any nation, it is both the expression and the interpretation of the life of the people concerned, revealing its ideals and aspirations, as seen through the eyes of its poets. The picture of present-day Icelandic literature as here presented is of course not complete, as several leading poets and prose writers have had to be omitted for lack of suitable selection, and following the tradition of this series, fragments of longer works have been excluded. The essay and the drama—and there are a number of notable examples of both in Icelandic literature of today—have had to be left out of the reckoning. All of which gives added force to the observation that literature flourishes abundantly these turbulent days in the modern and progressive Land of the Sagas.

The editor and publishers wish to express their gratitude to the translators for their generous permission to use their work, particularly to Mrs. Mekkin Sveinson Perkins, Mrs. Jakobina Johnson, and Professor Watson Kirkconnell, whose translations constitute such a large part of the volume. Thanks are also expressed to Mr. Thórhallur Bjarnarson, publisher of *Icelandic Lyrics* for cooperation.

RICHARD BECK

Bjarni Thorarensen

BJARNI THORARENSEN (1786–1841) is a central figure in modern Icelandic literature, for he was not only the pioneer Romantic poet in Iceland, but also the first great writer of the new and flourishing era in Icelandic letters which began during the earlier part of the last century. The scion of a prominent family, which included men of literary ability as well as leaders in national affairs, he studied law and held high judicial and governmental positions in Iceland. It is, however, Thorarensen the poet, not the distinguished and successful public man, who occupies a permanent place of honor in the history of his country.

He grew up at Hlídarendi, the historic home of Gunnar, hero of Njáls Saga, in southern Iceland, a region abounding in hallowed memories, and rich in scenic beauty which impressed him deeply and is reflected in his writings. His poems, contained in one rather slight volume, more than make up in quality what they lack in numbers. They are generally characterized by originality of thought and style, virility, and rich imagery, which is all the more remarkable in view of the fact that they are very largely occasional in nature. He excels in obituary, patriotic, and love poems. Rarely equalled in penetration, he further possessed the ability to clothe his thoughts in striking language. His stirring patriotic poem, "Eldgamla Ísafold," written when the author was eighteen and a student in Copenhagen, soon became the Icelandic national song, and still remains popular.

WINTER

TRANSLATED BY VILHJALMUR STEFANSSON

WHO rides with such fury
A fiery charger—
Through the high heavens
A horse snow-colored?
The mighty steed
From his mane tosses
Frozen flakes
That flutter earthward.

Glowing glitters
His gray armor;
On his shoulder there hangs
A shield ice-covered;
On his head he wears
The helm of terror—
The fearful Aegis'
Frosty helmet.

He comes from the hoary
Haunts of Midnight
Where the world force flows
From the well eternal;
Where restless seas
Roar in breakers
On shores without spring
And summer-less rocks.

He knows not of age
Though the oldest gods

Were his playmates ere
The earth was fashioned;
The last world will die
And desolation
Veil the suns
Ere his way is ended.

The strong are strengthened
When his step approaches;
The soft Earth grows firm
In his fierce embraces,
The tears she wept
Are turned to diamonds
And her mourning garb
To a mantle of ermine.

'Tis not truly said
That when summer approaches
Winter flees
To the frozen Northland:
He broods in the heavens
While humble spring
Leads summer in
Through sunlit meadows;

'Tis in his hands
The earth turns daily,
In his powerful grasp
The poles are twirling;
And he leaves,

E'en a little moment,
Naught of earth
That's near to heaven;

'Tis therefore we see
While summer lingers
The mountains still wear
The Winter's livery;
'Tis therefore we see
That summer melts not
Heaven's hoar-frost
From the head of age.

LINES TO SIGRÚN

TRANSLATED BY WATSON KIRKCONNELL

You vexed me with your vainness
Of view just now, my Sigrún.
I bade you boldly seek me
If borne from life before me—
And falsely you affirmed then
That feebly I would kiss you,
Claimed that I would not clasp you
When cold and pale and shrouded.

The maiden surely mocks me:
Remembrance would be fleeting
If, as she feigns to fancy,
I'd fail to love her phantom.

Your lips as your own would linger
Though lacking warmth and sweetness;
Your cheeks would warm my vision
Though chill and white I saw them.

Clings not the snow, caressing,
To kiss the face of winter,
Even as scarlet sunshine
The summer-rose embraces?
Pale is the purest lily.
Pale are you as the snowdrift.
Must you be mantled poorly
Though mouth and cheeks grow pallid?

If blood of human blooming
Blench from your lips and vanish,
Breezes of deathless beauty
Would breathe on them still forever.
Fair as the face of angels
I'd find your cheeks unblemished,
As fresh and fine as I knew them
Though the flame of life were ashes.

Leave me not then, my loved one,
Alone in the world of sorrow
If you should flee before me
To the fold of eternal quiet.
Come when the frosts grow keener
Cold in the autumn gloaming!
Come when the moon of midnight
Is masking its face in fog-murk!

Then may that moon in mercy
Remove from its pallid forehead
Its veil, when I see you vivid,
A vision that smiles upon me.
Follow, O follow, my fair one!
Float on a cloud to claim me!
Touch me in tender pity
With tips of your soft white fingers.

So when my ardor answers
And I open my arms to hold you,
Cast then your cold white bosom
Quickly upon my heart, dear!
Press on my pulses closely,
Press till your passion shall loosen
My soul from the flesh and its fetters
To follow you upward forever.

Then gladly we'll glide through the infinite spaces,
Kiss with the gleam of the night on our faces,
Ride the Aurora and swim its light-billows
Rosy as flames in a heaven of blisses,
Dance in the star-shine that floods the abysses,
And slumber in love on the clouds' snowy pillows.

Jónas Hallgrímsson

THOUGH highly unlike in temperament and artistic expression, Bjarni Thorarensen and Jónas Hallgrímsson (1807–1845) are inseparably associated in the history of Icelandic letters as contemporaries and fellow Romanticists. The virile quality and rugged style of the former are, however, in sharp contrast to the sensitive lyric touch and simple, flowing style of the latter, whose mastery of pure and melodious Icelandic has not been surpassed.

He was one of the four progressive Icelandic students in Copenhagen who founded the annual *Fjölnir* (1835) for the purpose of arousing the Icelanders, improving their literary taste, and purging their native tongue of foreign corruptions. The far-reaching impact of this publication can in no small degree be traced to Hallgrímsson, who exhorted and inspired the Icelandic people with his interpretations of their glorious past at the same time as he pictured the beauty of their native land in his exquisite lyrics. With his nature poems he struck a new note in Icelandic literature, and these, no less than his patriotic poems, breathe a deep love of country as well as a sympathetic understanding of all that lives, from "the mouse under the moss" to "the sea gull on the wave."

Hallgrímsson became a force in the movement for the purification of the Icelandic language. He greatly enriched Icelandic poetry with new metrical forms and lifted it to a higher artistic level. His popularity is still undiminished and his influence on succeeding writers has been very great.

A GREETING

TRANSLATED BY JAKOBINA JOHNSON

THE balmy South a gentle sigh releases—
And countless ocean billows, set in motion,
Breathe to my native shores the South's devotion—
Where strand and hillside feel the kindly breezes.

O give them all at home my fondest greeting,
O'er hill and dale a sacred peace and blessing.
Ye billows, pass the fisher's boat caressing;
And warm each youthful cheek, ye south winds fleet-
ing.

Herald of springtime, thou whose instinct free
Pilots thy shiny wings through trackless spaces
To summer haunts to chant thy poems rare,

O greet most fondly, if you chance to see
An angel whom our native costume graces.
For that, dear throstle, is my sweetheart fair.

THE GOLDEN PLOVER

TRANSLATED BY WATSON KIRKCONNELL

GAY the little plover flew
Swooping up the morning blue,
Singing in the light:
"Praise the bounteousness of God!

See how green is every clod,
See how heaven is bright!

"On the heath I have a nest,
Where my little babies rest,
Waiting me at home;
Them my mother-love supplies
Tender worms and pretty flies,
When once more I come."

Home the little plover sped
(Radiant shone the sun o'erhead,
Sweet earth's flowery floor)
Laden sought her nestlings small—
But the crows had crunched them all
Half an hour before.

Grímur Thomsen

THE career of Grímur Thorgrímsson Thomsen (1820–1896) was most unusual, ranging from many years of distinguished achievement in the Danish governmental and diplomatic service to the life of a country gentleman in his native land. It was after his retirement from public service abroad to the historic estate at Bessastadir in southern Iceland—his birthplace—that he devoted himself primarily to the writing of poetry.

At the University of Copenhagen, where he matriculated at the age of seventeen, he studied aesthetics and philosophy; these studies bore fruit in a prize essay on French literature and a thesis on Byron for which the author was granted his master's degree and later a doctorate. His review of H. C. Andersen's works (1855) was the first appreciative evaluation in Danish of that great genius. All this gives an inkling of Thomsen's wide reading, which was just as extensive in ancient as in later literature. Among his numerous translations into Icelandic the most important are his renditions from Greek lyric poems and tragedies.

Significant as his translations are, his own poems remain, however, his principal contribution. The historical and narrative ones are most characteristic. He succeeds admirably in recapturing the spirit of the past and in portraying men and women of heroic mold. His nature descriptions are also vivid and highly personal in style. Despite his long sojourn abroad, or perhaps rather because of it, he is profoundly Icelandic.

KING SVERRIR

TRANSLATED BY EIRÍKUR MAGNÚSSON

THE Pope and Prelate notwithstanding,
Listen to a king commanding:
Let my deathbed be the throne.
Crown'd I am, and none shall stay me,
Crown'd, till in the tomb ye lay me,
'Spite them all I reign alone.

Many were the hours of danger,
When I, famish'd and a stranger,
Trod a cold and distant shore;
But what were these to hours of anguish,
Banish'd for my home to languish,
All for fatherland I bore.

In my robes of state array me
When in death to rest ye lay me,
Bare my face alone shall be,
Vict'ry banner o'er me lying,
Serve the King as wings for flying
Onward to eternity.

Psalms it well behooves you singing,
And also set the bells a-ringing,
While in the mold ye make my bed.
One more boon I beg, however,
Blow the "Wakeful" * loud as ever,
Wakeful was the life I led.

* "Wakeful" was Sverrir's famous battle-trumpet.

ICELAND'S SONG

TRANSLATED BY JAKOBINA JOHNSON

HEAR the geysers in the highlands,
Hear the swans among the islands:
  That is Iceland's song.
Streams through rocky channels sweeping,
Falls through narrow gorges leaping:
  That is Iceland's song.

Song birds 'round the shores abounding,
Lofty cliff and cave resounding:
  That is Iceland's song.
Roaring breakers shoreward crashing,
Rushing winds like spirits flashing:
  That is Iceland's song.

Deep within my bosom's keeping
Rest these sounds of nature sleeping,
  That is Iceland's own.
Breathes through every great emotion
Joy, or sorrow's troubled ocean
  Iceland's softest tone.

Benedikt Gröndal

BENEDIKT SVEINBJARNARSON GRÖNDAL (1826–1907) was one of those rare individuals whom nature endows with almost unlimited versatility: scholar, scientist, artist, and poet. He grew up in an atmosphere highly favorable to the development of his literary genius, under the guidance and influence of his eminent father, the philologist Sveinbjörn Egilsson (1791–1852) who was also a poet of considerable ability, but above anything else the unrivalled master of Icelandic prose, as revealed in his translations of Homer.

Gröndal was a gifted and productive lyric poet, but his poetry is uneven in excellence, although he wrote some notable historical poems and shorter lyrics of a high order. He was a Romanticist to the extreme, and this constitutes his weakness as a lyric poet. His fertile imagination carries him so far afield that his poems very frequently become a veritable jungle of imagery, vague and even obscure. His lofty style, fluent and idomatic though it is, also tends to be excessively flowery.

His prose works are more interesting and significant, especially his masterful *Heljarslódarorusta* (1861), a rollicking burlesque on the battle of Solferino, which is unmatched in Icelandic literature.

REGRET

(*Hret*)

TRANSLATED BY JAKOBINA JOHNSON

ROSES and lilies have wilted away,
Summer skies changed to a shadowy gray.
Dreary the forest and leafless the trees,
Proudly that swayed in the wandering breeze.

Naked and moaning the trees meet the gale,
Still lies the brook in a desolate vale.
Gone from the heavens the warm tears that flow,
—Changed by the frost into hailstones or snow.

Gone art thou likewise, and dry with my years,
Lovéd and comforting fountain of tears.
Blessing and soothing—a world-healing force,
Thou wert a boon from a heavenly source.

Soft as the dew was thy touch on my cheek,
Solace and friend that our childhood may seek.
Peace would re-enter and sorrow depart,
Anger and pain would die out in my heart.

Soft rests the dew on the flowers at morn,
Down to the earth by its weight they are borne.
Looking again when the sun travels high,
Pure and refreshed to the beautiful sky.

Thus when the sorrows brought night to my heart,
Tears, like the dewfall, would heavily start.

Few were my years, and that dewfall in truth,
Driven away by the sun of my youth.

Out on the moors in a wintery gale,
Tears falling warm prove of little avail.
—Only our youth knows that sudden relief,
Flowery season—in passing too brief.

Heavenly Father, my childhood restore,
Make me contented and carefree once more.
Grant me those tears with their comforting flow,
—Grant that they change not to hailstones or
snow.

IN ABSENCE

TRANSLATED BY WATSON KIRKCONNELL

I SIT forsaken in the evening chill
And gaze upon the girdling silver seas
Now rising with the rising southern breeze
Beyond the bay where dim blue waves lie still.
All hail, fair wind, and hail, thou radiant light
That bringest hope beyond the darkening west!
And hail to thee, thou fairest maid and best,
Who now art hid behind the hills of night!
Ah, maiden, I shall guard thee in my thought
And ever hold thee close in memory,
Thou tender sweetheart I have loved so long.

With thee my midnight dreams are warmly
fraught;
And when the sun at dawning calls to me,
My waking heartstrings worship thee with song.

Páll Ólafsson

IT has been said of Páll Ólafsson (1827–1905) that he "represents in perfection the best qualities of the unschooled Icelandic poet" (Sir William A. Craigie), and no characterization could hit the mark better. For it is when writing in the vein of such Icelandic peasant-poets as Sigurdur Breidfjőrd and Bólu-Hjálmar that he has produced his most characteristic work. He possessed exceptional spontaneity and a rare skill in verse-making, with the result that many of his verses and songs still live on the lips of the Icelandic people and will no doubt continue to do so. That is equally true of his humorous and satirical pieces and no less of his charming love poems and effective convivial songs. Generally speaking, he is, however, at his best in his epigrams. His unusual ability in improvisation made him a master of the Icelandic quatrain, which became his vehicle for sundry themes, not least wit and deadly satire.

THE HAPPY VALLEY

TRANSLATED BY WATSON KIRKCONNELL

I INTEND to slip away
  To our Happy Valley,
Where the sun is ever gay,
  Where no dark clouds dally:
There all hearts are always light,
  Gladness comes to greet me,
There no winter, snow, or night
  Ever dares to meet me.

See how radiant is the land
  In rosy sunlight gleaming!
Let thy loving eye expand
  O'er all the valley dreaming!
See the waters, silver-white
  Where flocks of swans are oaring;
See the glittering mountain-height
  Above the green slopes soaring.

See the leas and uplands flash,
  Set with golden flowers;
See the groves of mountain ash,
  Where the cliff-side towers
Far beyond the leafy reach
  Of the oak tree's summit,
Far beyond the touch of each
  Drifting smoke-wreath's plummet.

Down the dark blue precipice
  Falls the foaming river,
Gulch and grove in thunderous hiss
  Laugh and groan and quiver.
Here is light and peace and calm,
  Life and birds' rejoicing;
Here I find my spirit's balm,
  Here my dreams come poising.

I have a Vale of Happiness,
  The world cannot behold it,
Its secret ways no one may guess,
  My heart will ne'er unfold it.

No others walk its shady grove
    Or come its streams to gaze on,
Because that Valley of our Love
    Is far too dear to blazon.

Steingrímur Thorsteinsson

STEINGRÍMUR THORSTEINSSON (1831–1913) was both a distinguished scholar and a productive creative writer. A philologist by training, he was for years a teacher of classics and modern languages in the State College of Iceland at Reykjavík and later (1904–1913) rector of the College, but at the same time he carried on his extensive literary work, which reflects the versatile scholar no less than the poet and patriot.

He greatly enriched Icelandic literature with his numerous and excellent translations in verse and prose, including *The Arabian Nights*, Shakespeare's *King Lear* and Andersen's Fairy Tales. His own poems have enjoyed unusual popularity and are still in high favor among many of his countrymen. From an artistic point of view, his nature and love lyrics, and in particular his satires and masterly epigrams, constitute his best poems. With his large number of lyrics written to popular tunes, which are probably sung more often than those of any other Icelandic poet, he contributed greatly to the development of vocal music in Iceland.

SWANSONG ON THE MOORLANDS

TRANSLATED BY JAKOBINA JOHNSON

ALONE, upon a summer's eve,
I rode the dreary moorlands.
—No more the way seemed bleak and long

For sudden strains of lovely song
Were borne across the moorlands.

The mountains glowed with rosy light.
—From far across the moorlands
And like a sacred interlude
It fell upon my solitude,
That song upon the moorlands.

It thrilled my soul with sweet response,
That song upon the moorlands.
As in a dream I rode ahead—
And knew not how the moments fled,
With swans upon the moorlands.

AT SUNSET

TRANSLATED BY JAKOBINA JOHNSON

Daylight is waning, dewdrops are shining,
Light sleeps the thrush in the blossoming dell.
Silent the breezes, sunlight declining
Smiles from the mountains a loving farewell.
Heavenly sunlight, do not forsake us,
Hallowed is evening with thee in sight.
Kindle our hopes ere darkness o'ertake us,
—Leave in our hearts thy dying light.

Glorious sunlight, thy failing power
Nature shall mourn with a dewfall of tears.
Say to each spirit, say to each flower:

"Soon o'er these mountains my light reappears."
—Come holy sunset, devoid of sadness,
Joy shall spring from those tears of pain.
Sorrows of evening shall change to gladness
Hailed when thy splendor breaks again.

VOICE OF SONG

TRANSLATED BY JAKOBINA JOHNSON

Come, soft and soothing—
Angel voice of song.
Anguish and sorrow
I have suffered long.
Soft as tears or falling rain,
Lightly touch my heart in pain,
As to flowers
Evening showers
Dying hopes restore.

Sweet as by fountains
Wooing birds may sing,
Deep as the echoes
Ocean winds may bring,
Let thy measures ebb and flow—
And my soul enraptured go
Swanlike sailing,
—Dreams prevailing—
On thy waves of sound.

A LOVE SONG

TRANSLATED BY JAKOBINA JOHNSON

A touch of the gold of thy tresses,
A look in the blue of thine eyes—
"And therein," my heart sang triumphant,
"My heaven of happiness lies."

I felt of thy cheeks' burning crimson,
Thy lips meeting mine in a kiss,
And therein my heart gained forever
Its lasting conception of bliss.

And love in our hearts was a captive—
Alas but a moment's respite,
A moment so golden and dazzling—
And then it was changed into night.

At eve when the dewdrops are gleaming,
With rays shed from stars in their course,
I know that the moment reflected
Its joy from a heavenly source.

EPIGRAMS

Generosity

TRANSLATED BY VILHJALMUR STEFANSSON

If you would do good, then do it today,
Do it gratis nor linger around for your pay:
Let the deed be a gem that you cast overboard,
Not a hook that is baited to fish for reward.

Lions and Swine

TRANSLATED BY VILHJALMUR STEFANSSON

The lion oft hungers, and yet,
Though the swine are well fed, and all that,
Higher the desert is set
Than the sty where the others grow fat.

Mountain and Hillock

TRANSLATED BY JAKOBINA JOHNSON

A lowly hillock raised its head
And to a lofty mountain said:
"Your innate pride and haughty mien
Are rueful in the distance seen."
The mountain neither moved nor spoke.
It knew not who the silence broke.

Matthías Jochumsson

FOR half a century Matthías Jochumsson (1835–1920) held a place as the leading poet of Iceland, highly esteemed by his countrymen. He was a clergyman and a versatile and prolific writer—a journalist, an essayist, a dramatist, and a lyric poet. His prose writings, such as his several travel books, are written in a lively, poetic style; his numerous letters, of which a large volume has been published, also eloquently bespeak the master of language. In literary significance his dramas rank far below his best lyric poetry, although his first play, *Útilegumennirnir* (The Outlaws) better known as *Skuggasveinn*, has remained a popular play down to the present day.

Jochumsson's poetry deals with a great variety of themes. His nature poems are impressive in their grandeur. His poems on subjects from the history of Iceland are particularly noteworthy. He has also written some of the most inspired and beautiful hymns in the Icelandic tongue—hymns where deep and abiding faith and rare spiritual insight are transmitted into the purest gold of lyric poetry. His truly inspired hymn, "Ó, Gud vors lands," written in 1874 for the millennial celebration of the settlement of Iceland, has deservedly become the Icelandic national anthem. In language and metrical forms he spans the centuries of Icelandic literature, harmonizing the old and the new. His numerous excellent translations include Shakespeare's *Hamlet*, *Macbeth*, *Othello*, and *Romeo and Juliet*; Byron's *Manfred*; Ibsen's *Brand*, and Tegnér's *Frithiof's Saga.*

THE MILLENNIAL HYMN OF ICELAND

TRANSLATED BY JAKOBINA JOHNSON

OUR country's God! Our country's God!
We worship Thy name in its wonder sublime.
The suns of the heavens are set in Thy crown
By Thy legions, the ages of time!
With Thee is each day as a thousand years,
Each thousand of years but a day.
Eternity's flow'r, with its homage of tears,
That reverently passes away.
  Iceland's thousand years!
Eternity's flow'r, with its homage of tears
That reverently passes away.

Our God, our God, we bow to Thee,
Our spirits most fervent we place in Thy care.
Lord, God of our fathers from age unto age,
We are breathing our holiest prayer.
We pray and we thank Thee a thousand years
That safely protected we stand;
We pray and we bring Thee our homage of tears—
Our destiny rests in Thy hand.
  Iceland's thousand years!
The hoarfrost of morning which tinted those years,
Thy sun, rising high, shall command!

Our country's God! Our country's God!
Our life is a feeble and quivering reed;

We perish, deprived of Thy spirit and light
To redeem and uphold in our need.
Inspire us at morn with Thy courage and love,
And lead through the days of our strife!
At evening send peace from Thy heaven above,
And safeguard our nation through life.
 Iceland's thousand years!
O, prosper our people, diminish our tears
And guide, in Thy wisdom, through life!

ECSTASY

FREELY RENDERED BY CHARLES WHARTON STORK

By the might of the spirit uplifted sheer
I was borne to the mountain's crest;
And my soul was a spring, so cool and clear,
Apart from the world's unrest.

From the crags all around, as I forced my way,
There were voices that screamed for my blood,
There were trolls mid the mist at their perilous play,
Till high on the summit I stood.

I had suffered, it seemed, the bitterest pain
That flesh ever lived through before;
But the danger now done, I was strong again,
And my poor heart trembled no more.

Sweet air I drank in, like one of the blest,
I was swimming on waves of power,
And every seed in the dark of my breast
Was quickened with gold that hour.

But the while my senses were still distraught,
My tranquil spirit was free,
And I heard strange harp notes within me,
wrought
As of manifold minstrelsy.

PROVIDENCE

TRANSLATED BY JAKOBINA JOHNSON

WHAT is that light, which points the way for me—
The way where mortal eyes no light can see?
What is that light, on which all light depends
And with creative power through space descends?
What writes of "love" on youth's illumined page
And "life eternal" on the brow of age?
What is thy light, thou fond and cherished Hope,
Without which all the world would darkly grope?
That light is God.

What is that voice I hear within, through life,
That echoes through our ranks of common strife?—
A father's voice, in wisdom to appraise,
A mother's voice, to comfort all the race.
What voice alone attuned perfection sings,
When all our world of song discordant rings?

Turns into day the darkness of the throng,
And agonies of death to hopeful song?
That voice is God.

What mighty hand maintained protecting hold
Upon this reed, through direst winter cold?
And found my life, a dormant wind-tossed seed,
And planted it, supplying every need?—
The hand whose torch must touch the sun with light,
Whose shadow means calamity and night.
The hand whose law has written its control
Upon each lily and eternal soul?
That hand is God.

NEW YEAR'S HYMN

ADAPTED BY KEMP MALONE

WHAT message bears the New Year sun?
He heralds nature's Christmastide:
He brings us life, and hope new won,
And grace of God, that shall abide.

As Jesus went about, of old,
So goes the sun his yearly round,
And cloaks his children from the cold
And comforts them for every wound.

O look upon his pathway bright,
Thou child that wouldst from winter flee,

And wheresoe'er the sun gives light
Lo! 'tis thy father seeking thee.

Fear not, though here be cold today
And worldly joys a feast foredone
And all thy strength as driven spray,
For God is Lord of earth and sun.

He hears the tempest's minstrelsy,
He hears the sleeping babe draw breath,
He hears the very heart of thee
And knows each throb from birth to death.

Ay, God is Lord in every age:
He speaks, His creatures but give ear.
His words excite, His words assuage
The mighty deep, the secret tear.

Within the hollow of His hand
Lie cradle, home, life's pathway, grave,
The weal, the woe of this our land
From topmost peak to utmost wave.

O may Thy succor be our sun
And hallow us for this new year.
O Lord most high, O Holy One,
O living God, we pray Thee, hear.

Kristján Jónsson

THE saying, "Those whom the gods love, die young," applies to few poets more strikingly than to Kristján Jónsson (1842–1869). This richly gifted farmer's son and farm laborer from northern Iceland was indeed a poet of great promise, but he died before reaching full maturity, at the early age of twenty-seven. Nevertheless, some of his lyrics are on a high poetic level in thought and form alike. Melancholy and pessimistic in tone, they mirror touchingly the adverse circumstances which were his lot, which wounded his soul, and thwarted his high hopes. His popularity is attested by the fact that his collected poems have run through four editions.

THE WATERFALL (DETTIFOSS)

TRANSLATED BY RUNÓLFUR FJELSTED

No sun-kissed golden-hearted flower
Among the boulders gray can wake;
White billows in terrific power
The cliff with feet of fury shake,
Where thou, old friend, art loud intoning
Forever thy tremendous lay;
Before thy wrath the rocks are groaning,
As reeds in gusts of dying day.

Thy odes arise of heroes vanished
And mighty men of former days;
Thou speakest much of freedom banished

And former fame's departing rays.
Above thee flames a glory gleaming,
That through the clouds comes sifting down,
And rainbow hues resplendent streaming
Thy wild titanic billows crown.

O thou of rolling waters fairest,
Terribly, marvellously fair,
Resistless in thy might thou farest,
Through rocky solitudes and bare;
Things change, for joy's bright fairy dower
Forsakes the woeful heart of flame;
Unbroken bides thy fearful power;
Thou rollest onward just the same.

Hurricanes rise and fell the flowers,
And billows crest above the reef;
Roses of laughing summer showers
Fade in the killing frost of grief;
Tears, burning tears on haggard faces
Stream, for the heart can find no peace;
But always on thy current races
In laughter that will never cease.

Deep in thy billows I would slumber,
When at the last my life will fail,
And tears of grief shall none encumber
Over my body still and pale;
When with a dirge and lamentation
Forms may be bowed above a grave,
In mad, terrific exultation
Over me will thy laughters rave.

THE TEAR

TRANSLATED BY JAKOBINA JOHNSON

A blessed cooling fount thou art,
O gleaming, pearly tear;
Refreshing every human heart—
A balm where wounds appear.

Oh leave me not when grief holds sway,
Thou tender friend in need.
Thus human woes are borne away,
Though wounded hearts must bleed.

I weep and feel my hopes restored,
—A light from heaven I see.
My tears are numbered by the Lord,
My faith shall comfort me.

Jón Stefánsson (Thorgils Gjallandi)

JÓN STEFÁNSSON (1851–1915), who wrote under the penname of "Thorgils Gjallandi," is one of the most interesting and significant figures in the literary and cultural history of modern Iceland. This self-educated farmer, in Thingeyjarsýsla in the northeastern part of the country, is a striking illustration of the high cultural level which the farmers of that district had reached through their contact with the works of leading foreign authors of the time, made available by their Reading Society; and his advanced views reflect the liberal and progressive spirit stimulated by that reading.

Thorgils Gjallandi appeared as a full-fledged realist already in his first book, a small volume of short stories (1892) which are a frank and fearless attack on existing conditions. Much more important, from a literary point of view, is his novel, *Upp vid fossa* (By the Waterfalls), an authentic description of Icelandic country life, deeply felt and vividly related. Here are many impressive descriptive passages, and the characterization is well done. The approach to the subject matter is realistic as before, but much more mature and effective. The profound sympathy of the author for all living creatures, not least the domestic animals with which as a farmer he had been so closely associated, is the strong undercurrent in his many appealing and masterly stories of animals, of which "Homesickness" is a memorable example.

HOMESICKNESS

TRANSLATED BY MEKKIN SVEINSON PERKINS

ALTHOUGH it is almost thirty years since I visited Hvanna Springs, an incident that happened to me and my companions there keeps constantly recurring to my mind in both my waking and sleeping hours.

There on a small gravel knoll to the southwest of the springs we saw the bleached white skeleton of a horse. This, we agreed, must be the remains of a runaway horse or a wild mountain horse which had met its death there. We made various guesses as to the fate and death hour of the animal, until our thoughts were diverted to the journey and to other things demanding our attention.

Since then both my waking and sleeping thoughts have often wandered to that gravel knoll and the white skeleton.

Now a short story has been made of it. I have combined my dreams and filled in the gaps. By this time I can scarcely distinguish that which I experienced in sleep from that which I have added while awake.

And this is the story.

Over the bright green pastures to the south of the homefield * at Brekka a herd of horses was scattered. A gentle south breeze stirred the slender tufted grass, and the leaves of the brushwood trembled in sympathy. Red, golden, and happily smiling, the aurora made the sign of the cross over the valley and gave life its blessing.

There were thirty horses in the herd. Hungry and gaunt after the long journey, they tore the grass and ate

* In front of an Icelandic farmhouse is a large cultivated grass plot known as the *tún* or homefield.

it voraciously. They would wander over the field, roll and shake themselves, and then attack the grass again with the same eagerness.

Two youths were watching the herd. They had been awakened two hours earlier to care for the horses of the traders from Skagafjördur, who had at last arrived. All spring the boys had looked forward to this day. They found it no hardship to get up early for this work and were in fine spirits as they ran among the horses, examining them all with care and now and then mounting one.

Some of the horses were untamed, others very skittish. These were the most likely to stray and the hardest to manage, and because they were unbridled the boys could not control them. There was one mare who was the liveliest and most restless of them all. Obviously she longed to escape, for again and again she tried to make her way west to the river, which roared northward through the valley, its swift current gray with glacial mud. The river was not easy to cross, yet the boys thought the sorrel mare with the light mane and the star on her forehead would not hesitate to rush into it if she had the chance.

"She's the most beautiful of all the horses," said the elder of the two boys. "I'd rather have her than any other, though she *is* hard to manage."

"Me too," said the younger. "I wonder if she's the one papa's to get?"

"I do hope so. But wouldn't it be nice to have the money to buy her? She'll be a fine horse, I'll wager! See, how she flies ahead of all the others."

"Yes, of course, she'll be fine, and papa will buy her, I'm sure." They both stared at Stjarna as, with flowing mane, she ran ahead of the young colts over the grassy plain to the horses grazing in peace on the mountainside above it.

By noon the horse traders had risen and, after breakfasting, they went out to the horses, followed by all the men of Brekka. This was a holiday for the farm hands, an occasion to which they had long looked forward.

"Which horse do you intend for me, my dear Thorkell?" asked the farmer, examining the herd with care.

"Take your choice, but I intended to offer you this one with the star on her forehead. I bought her specially for you."

"Unbroken, isn't she?"

"Not entirely; she's used to the halter. I mounted her two or three times on the trip and rode her a short distance. She will not disappoint you, but she has to be treated well."

"She is thin; has, of course, grown lean this spring."

"Yes, for she had a suckling foal. It was born in April and was given to another mare when I finally bought her. No horse of this breed ever fails."

"And the price?"

"Twenty-eight *spesiur*.* You get her for the same price I paid."

"That seems high. Twenty-five is quite enough for an unbroken six-year-old dam. Didn't you say she's a six-year-old?"

"Yes, I am sure of that. As for the price, I've been offered thirty, but you may have her for twenty-eight. Or you may choose from the herd."

They then caught Stjarna, and the farmer saddled her,

* Spesia (plural spesiur) is an old coin worth about $1.10.

after which he and Thorkell rode south over the plain. At the completion of the test, the farmer bought the mare, making his sons very happy.

"She may be inclined to run away; watch her carefully while she's getting used to the horses and pastures," said Thorkell, stroking Stjarna's neck. "I hope you have the same good luck with her that you had with old Skagi. I'll guarantee she's a fine horse."

"The river will prove an obstacle, I believe, and we'll watch her well," replied the boys' father.

Presently the horse traders prepared to depart. They left Brekka shortly before six o'clock that evening.

Stjarna was shut up in the stable with the farm horses while her former masters were getting out of sight. Later, someone who went out to the stable heard squealing and the thunder of trampling feet. Everything was in confusion. Stjarna was fighting old Kinna with such fury that the horseshoes rang and the stone walls reverberated. Most of the horses teased Stjarna. Being both agile and a hard fighter, she refused to give in.

The next week all the horses were hobbled. But the hobbles wore bad sores on Stjarna's feet; unlike the rest, who were used to them, she could not hop about.

Sunday morning the horses were driven home and into the corral. Then preparations were made for going to church. The farmer saddled Stjarna; this was an opportunity to try her out.

There being no prohibition law in those days, the men of Brekka refreshed their souls with the word of God and their bodies with liquor. When they reached home, they were both tipsy and happy, getting there just before bedtime. But their horses were quite warm. The day had brought them no rest and little happiness, either in the corrals or when tied to the stones.

Hard riding had not daunted Stjarna's spirits. In the morning she had run faster than any other horse, but as the day wore on she lost every sprint to Snaeringur. This was not strange, as he was in the prime of life, an exceptionally strong and reliable steed. But it was a great disappointment to Stjarna's new owner; Stjarna had made such a promising start.

"She'll not run away tonight even if she is left loose. Tired and hungry as she is, she'll be glad to rest; besides, she's now getting reconciled to the other horses," said the farmer, taking the bridle off the mare and patting her cheek. He then freed all the horses and went to bed.

The men of Brekka slept soundly and well that night. They rose later than usual Monday morning—to find Stjarna gone. She has never been heard of since. Extensive searching proved futile, and the farmer reproached himself with carelessness, while his sons wept bitter tears.

After the horses had rolled and grazed for a while, Stjarna left the herd and trotted down to the river. It did not prove a great obstacle to her, though the current was strong and the water cold and deep. The steep bank delayed her only a trifle; yet it had entirely stopped many a heavy hack horse and put him in a lather of sweat. Homesickness carried her swiftly across; escape to her was a fair wind.

She directed her course somewhat to the south of the trail, towards the herd of horses at home, the free mountain pastures, and the lovely lost colt. A loud neigh resounded—one only—and she ran silently westward, over gravel and rocky ridges, swamps and morasses. Mud-splashed and dirty, she rushed towards the desert, over barren lands and wastes and wilderness.

The vast glacial expanse shone in the sunlight. Kreppa, a dingy gray, flung itself northward, a river not easily crossed. The sorrel mare grazed a while on the green grassy plain to the east of it. Walking down to the river, she stuck her nose into the water and snorted three times, then turned away. Stjarna feared this foaming stream more than the Jökul River, when she first swam that raging torrent; morasses and marshes, deserts, barren wastes, and hunger had worn down her courage. She was afraid of this river.

A little farther north the stream widened out. There the current was not so swift, but on both banks were shifting quicksands. Stjarna paused for a time and smelled of the water; then she jumped in. Seized by the churning quicksands, she had to summon to her aid all her presence of mind and all her agility. This was a fight for life itself; the ordeal was terrific. She could not turn around, but managed to creep forward inch by inch. Terror gave her added strength. At last a sudden violent jerk, and the quicksands released their hold. Stjarna came blowing up from the depths and began swimming westward across the river. Head, mane, and shoulder tuft projected above the surface; the water barely covered her back. Stretching her head high, she set her teeth and expanded her nostrils, and her panting sounded sharp and hard above the murmur of the water. She swam gracefully, and it was lovely, that horse's head, with its keen expression and flashing eyes, gliding westward across the river.

On the western bank the quicksands were not so extensive, yet there, too, great exertions had to be made and terrifying ordeals faced before land was finally reached.

Then Stjarna ran for some distance to the southwest. She rolled for a long time in the sand, rose and shook herself, and set out again.

Soon after that she struck the lava field, the sharp, broken, rough lava field. She looked about for the best crossing. At the lowest and narrowest point brooks gleamed in the distance and green pastures spread before the eye. She started over the lava, stepping gingerly and smelling her way with care over the broken stony mass that often crumbled so treacherously under her feet. She trembled with fear; her heart beat fast and hard. The last stretch was the worst; there the rocks were largest and loosest and the crevices most numerous. But only a short distance remained, then the gravelly plain and finally the fragrant grass.

Pulling herself together, the mare continued over the hard rocky lava. The land here sloped downhill. She made a quick movement as the lava crumbled away from beneath her right fore foot. A sudden jerk and she would have escaped, but the edge of the mass broke with a crash from beneath her left hind foot, imprisoning it tightly in a crevice. Thrown flat to the earth, she lay thrashing about among the broken stones, in the wild frenzy of a sensitive creature, terrified to death. Blood streamed from both her cheeks; her wounds spread rapidly. As the slope was downhill, she tugged with her full weight at the foot that was caught. She jerked and struggled violently, resting only briefly now and then, in deadly anguish, the sweat of torture dripping off her in the broiling sun. Her eyes turned over in her head. Her panting and the hacking at the rocky mass broke the silence of the wilderness. At last a jerk was followed by a crash. The lava had crumbled away from around Stjarna's foot. She had only to stagger to her feet. She was free.

A miracle in the wastes and the silence of the wilderness—Stjarna had escaped alive. There at last she stood on three legs, bloody and trembling, on the gravel plain to the west of the lava field. She could no longer walk on her left hind foot; it was torn and ripped to shreds from fetlock to coronet—useless. A long time passed, filled with pain and loneliness; at last she set out, limping, westward towards the pastures.

The sun in the heavens, "God's eye," looking down upon all this, neither changed color nor swept away the cloud from before his countenance. He neither turned pale nor was shocked. The sun that shines on both the just and the unjust is raised far above the misfortunes and torments here below. He shines as hotly and brightly, though the children of earth weep and sigh and pray him for mercy. Whether man or beast is concerned, he remains unchanged.

There is no dearth of pasture at Hvanna Springs when the spring is fair and the summer fine. But the storms that come from the glacier are furious—driving winds with pouring rain, raging blizzards, and biting, piercing, glacial cold. That year the spring was early and exceptionally good. The summer was more capricious, especially th latter part of it.

By fall the sorrel mare, the lonely beast of Hvanna Springs, had grown lean. She was still very lame in her left hind foot, although her other wounds and injuries had healed. Her eyes were dull; her high spirits, her love of freedom, and her innate endurance were gone. The homesickness, mighty and sorrowful, alone remained, unimpaired and ever wakeful. Her eyes, once bright, sharp, and clear, had become clouded, dreamy, and tired, like the eyes of men who have suffered much and wept heavily. By fall she was a shadow of herself. She could no longer get home on three legs over the dangerous roads, no matter how hard the loneliness and exile were to bear.

The coming of fall brought storms and frost. The springs overflowed the best pastures along the streams and froze solid. Then winter with its heavy snows and ice laid a yet heavier hand upon the mare, bringing first want, then hunger, and lastly biting starvation.

On the morning of Twelfth-day, Stjarna stood on a certain gravel knoll surrounded by water which had rolled up over it and frozen in the bitter cold. A furious blizzard raged from the east. The mare turned her back to the wind and shook like a leaf.

Darkness fell and the moon waded through the clouds. It was dismal and ghostly on the point that night—nature was cold and stark, and the silence of death reigned. Onward the rivers rumbled mournfully, one in the east, the other in the west.

There stood Stjarna, shivering and drooping, until midnight. Then, raising her head, she looked long and steadfastly towards the west and saw the bright green pastures, the home of her youth and the horse herd, first hazily and at a distance, then ever nearer and nearer. The fragrance of the grass reached her nostrils. At last—at last she was coming home.

A sad, gentle happiness shone from her eyes, and they became sharp and sparkling as they used to be when the world was kind to her. It was lovely at home.

The vision moved forward to the glittering ice, over it and up to the knoll. The beautiful lost colt with the blonde mane led the herd. Stjarna jumped, intending to run to it, but in the movement she fell.

At that instant a whistling gust of wind rushed past. Death was passing by. It was he who helped Stjarna home. Then, as so often before, he became the angel of mercy to suffering worldlings, bringing peace and surcease of pain to the sick and the wounded.

Far from human habitation, on a barren basaltic knoll rest the bones of Stjarna, white and bleached. Wind and snowstorms, sunshine and showers pass over them day after day and year after year. Thither probably only few, besides myself, turn their thoughts.

But thoughts of that horse touch me deeply. Obeying the voice of her emotions and the mightiest yearning of her heart, she lost her way and walked the mysterious path. And for that reason she suffered and was tortured—alone, lost and forgotten, in the wastes and the wilderness.

Gestur Pálsson

Gestur Pálsson (1852–1891) was another of those writers of the last century who seemed definitely destined for literary greatness, and whose untimely death, therefore, was a great loss to Icelandic literature. A full-blooded realist according to the Brandes school, he was a journalist by profession, for a while (1890–1891) editor of the Icelandic weekly *Heimskringla* in Winnipeg, and an able essayist. He is, however, especially remembered for his well told tales dealing with contemporary life in Iceland. His first story of that kind, which appeared in the annual *Verdandi*, in 1882, showed him already a master of irony, and through his short stories generally his bitter pessimism and critical spirit are expressed in cutting satire, exposing the hollowness of time-honored convention, hypocrisy, and superficiality of every kind. His moral indignation is thus ever apparent in his works. Despite that fact, his deep human sympathy can readily be detected. His characters are primarily people who suffer in some way or other at the hands of society. In his stories there is traceable a definite influence from Alexander Kielland, the Norwegian novelist. Pálsson's verse is far inferior to his stories; the best of his poems are in a satirical albeit humanitarian vein, such as "Betlikerlingin" (The Beggar Woman).

THE TALE OF SIGURDUR THE FISHERMAN

TRANSLATED BY MEKKIN SVEINSON PERKINS

I

ALL my life I have greatly enjoyed travel, whether by land or sea. We Icelanders often feel that there is very little diversion to be had in this land of ours—and that is quite true. Yet there are few greater or more exhilarating pleasures than to ride on a fine horse over a good trail on a summer day with an entertaining companion at one's side.

When I think of pleasure trips of that kind, I always recall the one we took, Thorarinn and I, to a certain fishing village on the coast.

We were natives of the same district and were both in school at the time. Finding much pleasure in being together, we had long planned a trip to the village, which is about a day's journey from our home.

Finally, in the evening of a fair day in the month of July, we set out.

By the time we reached the mountain beyond which the village lay, it was almost midnight, but at that season of the year only a sort of twilight falls. One cannot deny that it is pleasant to be on a mountain trail on such a night when the skies are clear and the weather is fine.

Nowhere else can one so completely enjoy the beauties of nature as up in the mountains. Down in the valleys the work of man meets the eye on every hand; one cannot help feeling that his puny work is a blot, so to speak, on the gigantic book of nature; without it nature would be all the purer and more majestic. Up in the mountains, on the other hand, there is nothing to detract from the grandeur of nature. Nowhere is the stillness of a summer night so intense. Range upon range of majestic peaks, miles of desert wastes, endless vistas stretch out silently in all their majesty; there are only the trails to remind one of the work of man.

Thorarinn and I rode slowly along the mountain trail, drinking in the silence and the beauty of the summer night. We were in no hurry, and the trail was rather rough.

As we rode along we chatted of this and that, recalling ghost tales connected with the mountain, and especially with the public shelter there. Although we vied with each other in our condemnation of such superstitions, as a matter of fact we still clung to the beliefs of our childhood and would have been afraid to travel alone after dark. But we hated to confess such weakness. In the brightness of the summer night we could easily assume an air of bravado, especially as there were two of us. Thorarinn even went so far as to suggest that it might be good sport to stop at that ghostly haunt, the shelter, and see what it looked like inside.

But when we reached the shelter, we both whipped up our horses and galloped past in silence. Neither of us made any mention of dismounting, and the glance my companion gave it in passing bespoke anything but courage.

After that no further mention was made of ghosts. We hurried on. By the time we came to the lower reaches of the mountain the sun had been up for more than an hour. Behind us lay the mountain trail, while before us stretched a magnificent scene. The early morning sun shone in all its glory on surrounding peaks and hills, imparting a majestic beauty to this endless vista as it lay enveloped in complete silence. Down in the valley below us everything spoke of the eternal struggle for existence. Gradually, from chimney after chimney in the scattered farmhouses, smoke came curling up into the air, and here and there men were seen leaving home for their work in the fields.

We stayed overnight in a farmhouse at the foot of the mountain. By morning the weather had changed. Gone were the calm and the beauty of the night before. Instead, a wet sleet was falling and a piercing cold wind came directly from the Arctic ice which never left the harbor that year.

On seeing this, we hastily made preparations for departure and rode like mad to the village, arriving there by nightfall.

Having neither friends nor acquaintances in the village, we put up at the inn. After sprucing up a bit, we decided to go downstairs and have some refreshments before going out to take a look around.

We found the parlor dark. The shutters on the windows had been closed, and a fire had been kindled in the stove, the door of which stood open, sending a faint gleam of light across the floor and upon the gigantic form of a white-haired man seated on a bench. Hunched over a table, he sat there staring into the fire, unaware that we had entered.

Perhaps because of the darkness of the room, or because of the gigantic hulk of the figure before us, I shrank back. Yet there was no reason to be afraid, as we soon learned.

When the maid brought the light, I began to look more closely at the man. His features were coarse yet gentle, and a look of intense sorrow pervaded his whole being.

Obviously, he was quite tipsy; in one hand he clasped a tin mug, which he raised slightly toward the maid when she brought in the light, ordering her to fill it again.

The maid knew at once what he wanted. Taking the mug, she filled it with toddy and brought it to him. He received it in silence, placed it to his lips and drained it at one draught, then ordered more.

The maid filled the mug again. This time, instead of raising it to his lips, the man set it down on the table beside him.

We took seats at a table some distance from him. We intended asking about him when the maid came to take our order, but she hurried off before we could say a word.

For a long time the man sat there in absolute silence, not giving us so much as a glance. Then, of a sudden, he straightened up and placed one arm on the table. Never have I seen so large and muscular an arm. The muscles stood out like ropes as he clasped the tin mug in his hand. The man sat there, with head bent, staring straight into the fire.

We began whispering together, still keeping our eyes on the gigantic white-haired stranger. All of a sudden, we noticed that he seized the mug, drained it off at one draught, and let his head sink farther down on his chest. We thought he was about to drop off to sleep.

But then we saw that his lips were moving and we heard him whisper as if to himself:

"Cain! Cain!"

He repeated the words, this time in a loud voice:

"Cain! Cain!"

It was like a cry of despair. There was such terror in the voice that we were moved to pity.

In our excitement we may have accidentally knocked against the table, for all at once a shudder seemed to pass through the man's huge frame, he lifted his head and turned his eyes on us.

Never have I seen such sorrow and despair in any human eyes! It was as if grief had seared his very soul.

He struggled to get to his feet, but being too tipsy for that, was forced to sink back upon the bench. Laying his left arm down on the table, he dropped his head upon it, while in his right hand he held the tin mug as if in a dying grasp.

Soon after that we heard him snoring. On looking closer, we saw that he had crushed the mug between his fingers into a shapeless mass!

At that instant the innkeeper arrived, and we at once asked him who the stranger might be. "Sigurdur the Fisherman," replied the innkeeper, as if that ought to mean something to us.

"Has he crushed that one too?" went on the innkeeper, going over to the table at which Sigurdur was now sleeping and examining the mug more closely. "I tell you, I've been at my wit's end to get him something to drink from. He smashed every glass we gave him, often cutting himself, until finally I got these tin mugs specially for him. He usually treats them more gently."

"Isn't he a dreadfully quarrelsome fellow?" I asked.

"Sigurdur the Fisherman quarrelsome! On the contrary, he is one of the most peaceable of men, although he is strong enough. But surely you've heard of Sigurdur the Fisherman! Is it possible you haven't heard his story?"

We had to confess that we had never heard of him.

"His was a great tragedy!" went on the innkeeper, a look of gravity spreading over his usually smiling features.

Sitting down at the table with us, he then related the tale of Sigurdur the Fisherman.

II

THE fall season had been better than any within the memory of the oldest inhabitants. The fishing boats nearly always came in heavily laden, and the weather was remarkably fine, though rather changeable.

That season the best catches were invariably those of Sigurdur, who was just twenty at the time. He was considered the strongest young man in the whole countryside, as well as the ablest fisherman. He had just been placed in command of one of the boats and, as everyone said, was performing his new duties very well. A veritable giant of a man he was even in his youth, with exceptionally broad shoulders that were slightly stooped as he walked. Yet for all his bulk, he was good-natured and always calm and composed.

Sigurdur had a brother named Einar, one year his junior and a member of his crew. The two brothers differed in many respects. In contrast to Sigurdur, Einar was of slender build and in poor health, especially inclined to be weak-chested, and hence unable to do much hard labor. Despite this infirmity, he was a very active and cheerful young man and the greatest of wags.

Sigurdur, on the other hand, was rather reserved. He seldom took any part in the games so often played at the village. On days when rough seas kept the boats tied up, the sand hills out beyond the huts were crowded with fishermen engaged in all manner of sports. There were impromptu wrestling and boxing matches, and other contests of a physical nature. Words were bandied and even stones hurled if no suitable retort came to mind. And sometimes all those who were best versed in lays and rhymes would gather in one of the huts to play a verse-capping game. In fact, everything was done that a group of active young men can invent to help pass the time and make merry.

Although quite different in many respects, Sigurdur and Einar got on very well together. Sigurdur treated Einar more like a son than a younger brother. Whenever Einar was indisposed, as he often was, Sigurdur would show him the greatest consideration and give him the tenderest of care. Einar, in return, loved his brother dearly and looked up to him as the world's wisest man.

But there was one respect in which the two brothers were alike. They were both extremely superstitious, Sigurdur perhaps even more so than Einar, for he hardly dared walk through the house alone after dark. They were often teased about this weakness, Sigurdur in particular. It seemed odd that such a giant in strength should be afraid of ghosts. To this his usual reply was that it was no stranger for him to fear the supernatural than for Grettir the Strong of saga fame.

The brothers came by their belief in ghosts quite naturally. They had been reared in a part of Iceland where belief in the supernatural was, if possible, even firmer than elsewhere in that highly superstitious nation, at a time when superstition was rife. Throngs of itinerant ghosts known as Mórar haunted the region, and a multitude of their female counterparts, the Skottur, wandered abroad, seen and heard by everyone, both by those endowed with second sight and by those without that gift. This ghostly horde grew with almost every death. No sooner had the spirit left the body than it not only appeared to all relatives, friends, and neighbors, but wandered back and forth throughout the whole region. If someone left a home where a death had taken place, the shade of the departed always managed to follow him wherever he went, amusing itself by running on ahead to every farmstead and suddenly thrusting its ghostly countenance into the face of any unsuspecting person who chanced to be outside. Or it would climb up on the housetop, straddle the roof, and ride about up there. Then it would slide down to the ground, tie the cows in the stable together by their tails, put out the light in the kitchen, or with its icy hand stroke the cheek of some hired girl, almost throwing her into a faint. Or at times some member of the household, on sticking his fingers into his pouch for an innocent pinch of snuff, would suddenly strike ice-cold fingers already there, also on snuffing bent. Whenever any of these phenomena occurred, it was a sure sign either that a visitor from one of the many haunted farmsteads would soon arrive, or that some near relative or dear friend had passed on to the next world and was making the rounds to announce his departure.

From earliest childhood the brothers had grown up on stories of this kind. That they should be superstitious is therefore a matter of small wonder. Anything that seemed to have no possible explanation was usually ascribed to some ghostly influence. If a horse shied in the dark, it had, of course, seen something unclean; if a man lost his way at night or in a blinding blizzard, he had been led astray by an evil spirit; if some strange disease smote one of the domestic animals, a ghost was always blamed for it.

CHRISTMAS was coming, and all the fishermen whose permanent abode was elsewhere than in the fishing village were making ready to go home for the holidays.

As was their wont, Sigurdur and Einar planned to go home to their mother's and stay there until the opening of the winter fishing season. But on the day set for their departure, Einar fell ill, and the trip had, of course, to be postponed. Although Einar felt somewhat better the next day, he was hardly well enough to undertake the journey. Both young men fully realized that their mother would be worried if they put off their visit till after Christmas; they also knew that the start had to be made that very day if they were to reach home by Christmas Eve, for it was a two days' journey to their home. Einar was frantic to go. But having decided that he should remain behind, Sigurdur took him to the farmstead on the outskirts of the village and made arrangements to have him stay there till after

Christmas; by that time they hoped he would be well enough to proceed homewards.

Having seen to this matter, Sigurdur prepared to make the trip alone. His mother had sent a pack horse for the baggage; Sigurdur himself intended to go on foot, for the trails were still passable.

As for Einar, he was visibly moved when it came to the actual parting. Though downcast at the thought of being left behind, he felt compelled to yield to his brother's wishes.

On the first day the trail lay through a settled farming district, but on the second it wound its way across a deserted valley and up a barren mountainside. The weather was fine—clear, with tingling frost, when Sigurdur, leading the horse, set out from the fishing village. By nightfall he had reached a farmstead near the foot of the mountain that lay between him and his home. There he spent the night.

The following day was Christmas Eve. Sigurdur rose at the first faint streak of dawn. Though the weather was clear, his host urged him to wait till the sun had risen, that they might better judge the prospects for the day. But Sigurdur was impatient to be off. He knew that unless the start were made at once, he would hardly have time to cross the mountain before nightfall, and no one was less desirous of being on the road alone after dark. Considering these circumstances, Sigurdur set out at once.

Like any traveller up and on his way in the early morning hours of a splendid day, confidently expecting to reach home before dark, Sigurdur felt very light-hearted and cheerful as he strode towards the mountain.

A light gray morning mist covered the whole valley.

Little by little it lifted, bringing peaks and depressions gradually into view. And as the day dawned brighter, Sigurdur could see that the sky was clear, giving promise of fine weather.

At the point where the trail turned up the mountainside, Sigurdur came to a halt. Here he rested his horse awhile, allowing it to graze and giving it some of the hay brought from the farm where he had passed the night.

He took the opportunity to look around him. By this time the sun had risen. Before him the valley stretched, steel gray in the morning light, for it was not yet completely covered with snow. On either side of it rose the huge, jagged black cliffs that bordered the ravines; still farther up the early morning light caught the gleam of snowy ridges, and here and there lofty crags and peaks stood out oddly against the brilliant yellow of the eastern sky. Some leaned backward, as if, tired of a long and monotonous existence, they now wished to lie down and rest till Doomsday; others seemed to bend forward, as though peering down into the valley to see if any living creature could be so foolhardy as to come far up into the mountainous wastes to visit them.

Although he could not have put his feelings into words, Sigurdur fully appreciated the grandeur of the scenery before him. But, being a careful traveller, he now began to look more closely to the weather. Hardly a breath of air was stirring; the sky was clear, except for a light mass of clouds atop the highest peak at the very head of the valley.

After a short rest, Sigurdur started up the slope. The trail zigzagged its way in countless turns, up and up. So long and hard a climb it was that a traveller took as long to mount to the crest on a summer day as to ride all the way through the valley.

As Sigurdur climbed upward, he turned his gaze now and then to the cloud at the head of the valley. He soon saw that it was growing larger. In a moment it appeared to expand to many times its original size. Meanwhile more light clouds kept forming below it, until the peak at the head of the valley was completely enveloped. Before long, the lower peaks all around were also wearing their caps of fleecy white, which gradually spread down over them, growing denser and darker all the while.

On gaining the top of the first slope, where the upper reaches of the mountain came into view, Sigurdur at once observed that snow was falling up there. He could see the dense white masses whirling about, as though caressing one another and striving to work their way towards him. Down where he was a stiff breeze had risen and was blowing in his face. Fear clutched at his heart as he looked ahead, and the thought flashed through his mind, "How lucky that Einar didn't come along!"

For a brief moment Sigurdur considered turning back, but on second thought decided to push forward. He knew so well the trail that lay ahead, having crossed the mountain on many a stormy winter day, though, to be sure, never before alone. Thoughts of his mother also strengthened him in his resolve. She would be very anxious, he knew, if neither he nor Einar came home, especially as there was such a blizzard. And so, driving the horse before him, he hastened along the trail at a brisk pace.

But the swirling masses of snow on the mountainside

were gradually bearing down on him. Before long, they had overtaken him; the snow was falling all around him. Looking back, he could see that it was also snowing on the lower part of the trail. As he climbed, the snow closed in tightly on every side of him, constantly narrowing his field of vision. It pelted him in the face, whirled in eddies round him, then was driven onward by the ever-increasing fury of the gale. Soon he found himself completely enveloped by a dense, blinding mass of snow, whirling and eddying in the howling storm.

Sigurdur shuddered at the thought of the possible outcome of this journey. And it was not strange that he should. There is nothing more terrifying in this land of adversity of ours than to be out on a desolate mountain alone, in a howling blizzard. Up there no help is ever at hand. Alone, without seconds, nature and the wayfarer fight the duel to a finish, and if perchance some shriek of terror were sent out, the gale would snatch it at once and whirl it far out into the endless void, where it would soon die away.

Once more Sigurdur considered turning back, and once more decided against it. He knew far better the part of the trail that lay ahead than that over which he had just passed, across the valley and up the mountainside. But by this time the gale had waxed so furious that Sigurdur could no longer drive the horse ahead of him. The beast stopped dead in its tracks, and turning its rump to the wind, refused to budge, until Sigurdur was forced to walk on ahead and lead it by the rein.

The swirling snow had by now become so dense that Sigurdur could scarcely see a hand's breadth before him;

he nevertheless managed to keep to the trail, for it was well marked by cairns, the ground still visible in many places, only a little of the snow having settled as yet. But the higher Sigurdur climbed, the heavier became the snowfall, making it ever harder for him to see the trail, and worst of all, the snowflakes steadily pelting him in the face completely blinded him. Again and again he was forced to come to a halt and with the warmth of his hand endeavor to thaw away the snow and ice clinging to his eyelashes.

Sigurdur realized that only by the grace of God could he ever reach the shelter, and he made up his mind to pass the night there, though a cheerless Christmas Eve it would be. He had not strayed from the trail, of that he felt quite certain. But with every passing minute the storm grew worse, the raging wind more furious, the snowfall denser, the night darker. And the horse straining ever harder on the rein greatly slowed down the pace. At last the brute lay down and refused to go on. There were a few moments when Sigurdur feared he might never budge it again. At length, however, he did get it to its feet and off. The very next instant, in the blinding storm, he stumbled against a cairn which, on closer inspection, turned out to be the one beside the shelter. He then fought his way over to the shelter and went inside.

So many lives had been lost crossing the mountain that finally, after years of discussion, the districts on both sides of it decided to erect a shelter at this spot. Like most public buildings of its kind in the Iceland of those days, this one was very poorly built. When the welfare directors of the districts to the north and south received instructions from their boards to erect such a building at the expense of the two districts, more effort was made to find ways and means of making a little profit from the project, as from all public works, than so to construct and equip the shelter that it would best serve travellers who might seek refuge within its walls from the raging elements.

Despite this, the shelter, when new, proved adequate. It consisted of only a single room with a bunk built in at one end and a stall for the horses at the other. At first wood, a pot, a shovel and some matches had been placed beside the fireplace, and a little hay in the manger. But even before snow flew that very first fall all the hay had disappeared, not a stick of wood remained, and the matches were not to be found. After that, these articles were no longer supplied. Soon the shovel vanished. The pot hung on longest, but it, too, eventually disappeared one fall when the nights were beginning to lengthen.

The need for supplying more and better furnishings was, it is true, discussed at great length at the meetings of the district boards on both sides of the mountain, but no action was ever taken. The members of each board accused the inhabitants of the other district of having stolen the things from the shelter. Finally, one fall, the door disappeared. That was the last straw. The welfare director of the district to the south donated a new door, and that ended the matter.

After entering and looking about inside, Sigurdur shut the door. Fearing the wind might force it open, he piled his pack saddle and baggage against it, and used his staff as a further reinforcement. This done, he fed his horse and climbed into the bunk, which he had made as comfortable as circumstances permitted.

Sigurdur then closed his eyes and tried to sleep. But sleep would not come. Now that he was indoors, safe from the storm, and had the opportunity to rest, Sigurdur began to feel uneasy. No matter how hard he tried to shut them out, the ghost stories he had heard all his life came rushing into his mind. One after another they came, in an ever-growing train. The spectral figures took on life and paraded before him. He couldn't take his eyes off them. They held him spellbound till he sprang up with a start, uncertain whether what he saw was reality or merely a dream. He peered out into the darkness. Wasn't there something out there? No, he couldn't see a thing. He lay down again and the cold sweat broke out from every pore in his body.

Then he tried keeping his eyes open, turning his thoughts to other things and listening to the gale that howled around the shack. In his mind's eye he could see the snow-drift piling up against the wall outside. He lay there peering out into the darkness until spots of many colors began floating before his eyes—and there were the old ghosts back again.

Meanwhile, at the other end of the room, the horse was munching its hay as calmly as though at home before its own manger. The sound had a soothing effect on the nerves of the frightened man.

By this time Sigurdur's clothing was beginning to thaw out and chilled him to the marrow. Jumping down from the bunk, he thrashed about with his arms till his blood was somewhat warmed. Then, feeling a drowsiness creep over him, he climbed back into the bunk and once more tried to sleep.

A short time passed. The storm without seemed to abate a little. The horse had stopped munching the hay. To Sigurdur the darkness and the eerie stillness of that desolate shack, away up in the mountain wastes, far from all human habitation, seemed so awesome. Try as he might, he could not sleep. No sooner had he shut his eyes than thoughts of the many human beings who had perished on that very spot assailed him; some had barely managed to crawl inside the shelter to die. At thought of them, Sigurdur couldn't help opening his eyes and peering out into the darkness again to see whether their ghosts were not still lurking out there. And with that he was wide awake again. Restless and tense, he tossed to and fro.

All at once he thought he heard the sound of footsteps on the roof. Something seemed to sit down astride the ridge and ride along it slowly, very slowly. In a panic, Sigurdur raised himself on his elbow and listened more attentively. Yes, he could clearly hear the creaking of the timbers overhead.

At that instant, the horse, terrified at the sound, sprang up and came stumbling over to the bunk. Pressing its body close against the boards, it rested its head on the man's feet, which dangled over the edge.

Now came several thumps and thuds, so loud that all the timbers overhead creaked and groaned. It was almost as if someone were dragging across the roof a hide filled with heavy rocks. Next came a powerful blow on the door, followed immediately by several others.

By this time Sigurdur was quaking from head to foot. He could feel the horse, too, trembling in every limb. Thrusting its head still closer to the man, the terrified creature quivered and shook all over.

The weird rapping at the door continued off and on for some time, but as the night wore on the blows grew fainter and fainter, till at length they ceased entirely.

When at last all was quiet, Sigurdur jumped down from the bunk and wrapping both arms round the horse's neck, patted the creature gently until it ceased trembling. Then, leading it to the other end of the room, he lay down beside it. He began scratching together the leavings of the hay, and the horse began its munching again. Thus they lay together, the man and the beast, like two brothers, the remainder of that dreadful night—both equally frightened, both equally thankful for the companionship of another living creature.

Sigurdur did not sleep a wink that livelong night. When he thought day had dawned at last, he got to his feet and began to stir about. It took some time to remove all the baggage from before the door, but once that had been accomplished, Sigurdur jerked the door open and looked out.

His eyes fell on the form of a man lying outside, the face turned towards the door, the body half buried in snow. He gave but one glance at the face before him. That one glance was enough. He knew those features only too well, despite their ghastly pallor. They were the features of his brother Einar.

III

DURING the afternoon of the following day the weather changed for the better.

At Dalbotn, the farm nearest the mountain, suddenly the figure of a man was seen stumbling down the trail with a burden in his arms. It was Sigurdur the Fisherman carrying the body of his brother Einar. He had left the horse and baggage behind in the shelter.

In that one night his hair had turned white. At first he was like one in a stupor, unable to utter a word. Little by little, however, he recovered sufficiently to tell the tragic tale of the shelter on the mountainside.

For a long time Sigurdur was as if beside himself; in fact, he never entirely recovered from the shock. His fear of the dark grew so that it was never safe to leave him alone either in the house or outside after darkness had fallen; otherwise he would be upset for days.

When the sad news was broken to her, Sigurdur's mother took to her bed and died the following spring.

After her death Sigurdur sold the farm and moved to the seacoast, where he bought a hut and settled down to fishing the year round. He still retained his reputation as the best fisherman in those parts, usually having command of a boat.

He never spoke of the affair at the shelter and no one ever mentioned it in his presence. In fact, he seldom spoke at all unless spoken to; sometimes for days on end he would answer in monosyllables only.

When at sea he was somewhat more genial, especially in a raging storm. Then it was as if a load had been lifted from his shoulders; his eyes would rove in all directions, now to the waves, now to the wind, now to the sails, and a strange happy peace seemed to shine from his sorrowful, weather-beaten countenance. In these circumstances he was even known to joke with his men.

As time went on the story of Sigurdur was forgotten except by a few of the older inhabitants. He was considered by most a good-natured eccentric, best left alone, for if angered, he would be a hard fellow to tussle with.

In his hut the telling and reading of ghost stories was strictly forbidden. One day when he had come upon one of his men reading a book of Icelandic folk tales, which are mostly about ghosts, he had instantly snatched the book from the man's hands and thrown it into the fire. The subject was never broached again, but after that none of his men dared open such a book in his presence.

Then he took to drinking. At first lightly. He would take a glass whenever he went to the village, but never enough to show any effects.

Soon after that he was made pilot in the port. This new duty he performed with his usual conscientiousness and skill; he went out farther than any pilot ever had done and seldom failed to report even in the worst weather. But he drank more heavily than before, both because there was more opportunity for drinking and because the work was more fatiguing.

Sigurdur had a small two-oared boat, which he used for trips to the village when the weather was too bad for fishing and no ships were expected in the harbor. He would row up to the jetty below the inn, tie his boat, and make straight for the bar.

If there were many customers hanging around the inn, and especially if there was much of an uproar, he would turn back at once, go into one of the stores and buy a flask of brandy. Then he would row straight for home.

But if there were only a few customers at the inn, and especially if he was the only one, he would seat himself on a certain bench at a certain table across from the stove and begin ordering drinks.

At first he would sip his drink slowly, but after he had become somewhat intoxicated he would order one glass after another and drain it at one draught, until at last he fell asleep at the table, always with his head resting on his left arm and his right hand clasping the glass.

This became a habit. No one paid any heed though he fell asleep over his glass. He was left strictly alone. In the morning, when the innkeeper and the servants came down, he had usually disappeared, having crept out silently during the night and gone down to his boat.

IV

This was the story of Sigurdur the Fisherman as told us by the innkeeper.

My companion and I were restless that night; time and again we would wake up and begin talking, always about Sigurdur. We hoped he would still be at the inn when we got up in the morning, for we wished to take a closer look at him.

In this we were disappointed. By the time we got up Sigurdur had disappeared.

On our way home over the mountain trail we again

passed the shelter where this tragedy had occurred. Neither of us suggested dismounting and going inside to look about, even though it was broad daylight.

Many years passed.

At first my thoughts would often turn to Sigurdur, though less and less frequently as time went on, until I had completely forgotten him, when one day I had to take a trip to the village where I had seen him.

On arriving at the village, I made directly for the inn. It was then that the figure of Sigurdur rose so clearly in my mind that I could almost see him asleep at the table, his head resting on his left arm and the crushed tin mug clasped in his right hand.

The innkeeper came forward at once to greet me. His hair and whiskers had by this time turned almost white and his figure was somewhat shrivelled with age. But he was as jolly and talkative as ever. When I reminded him that I had stopped at the inn years ago, he remembered me at once and treated me like an old friend. He called his wife, whom I immediately recognized as the girl who had waited on us during our previous visit, though grown quite matronly with the years.

"Do you remember Sigurdur the Fisherman?" I asked the innkeeper.

"Of course I remember him," was the reply. "And now he is gone."

"Gone?" I asked.

"Yes, he was drowned last winter in the storm which wrecked four of our boats here in the harbor."

"And a great loss he was," interposed the innkeeper's wife. "The best customer we ever had; always paid his debts to the last *eyrir*."

"And his end, too, was dramatic," went on the innkeeper after a moment's silence.

When I had taken my refreshment, the innkeeper told me the end of the tale of Sigurdur the Fisherman.

As he grew older Sigurdur took to drinking more and more heavily. Sometimes he would be frantically wrought up, especially when drunk, and at times even delirious.

When at sea, he would sometimes frighten his men, who could only with difficulty handle him in these fits. Yet, despite the rumors that began to spread, he could get enough men to man his boat, for his catch was always fine.

That winter the weather had been very unfavorable, and consequently Sigurdur had time for many more trips than usual in his small boat to the village.

One day, on returning from one of these trips, somewhat the worse for liquor, he entered his hut to hear one of his men telling a dream. The man dreamt that he had been out fishing with Sigurdur when a frightful storm arose and swamped the boat, which sank just as he woke up.

On hearing this, Sigurdur turned to his men and recited the following verse:

> Though at last I am to drown,
> I have one consolation,
> Widow and children have I none,
> To weep in desperation.

In the discussion of dreams and their fulfillment which followed Sigurdur took no part.

The next day, the weather being fine, most of the fishermen went out, Sigurdur among them. Afterwards one of his men recalled that Sigurdur had seemed unusually depressed that morning.

Later, in the afternoon, a storm came up and the waves ran high before the landing. Most of the boats returned as soon as the storm rose, but Sigurdur refused to budge until long after the last of them had gone. By the time he finally made preparations for going ashore the gale was whistling all around the boat, whipping up a heavy sea.

Sigurdur was an exceptionally fine helmsman and never had his men known him to steer as expertly as he did that day. But on reaching the surf before the landing place, they were horrified to see him turn suddenly and stare into the surf. His features stiffened and he uttered a shriek of anguish: "Einar! Einar!" At that moment he let go of the tiller. The boat capsized instantly, throwing the whole crew into the sea. Only two of the men were rescued; Sigurdur went down with the rest.

Stephan G. Stephansson

STEPHAN G. STEPHANSSON (1853–1927) was born in northern Iceland and came of a poor but sturdy and intelligent farmer family; literary interest and marked poetic ability had characterized his forbears. At the age of twenty he emigrated with his parents to America, where he became three times a pioneer: first in Wisconsin, again in North Dakota, and lastly in Alberta, Canada, where he made his home from 1889 until his death.

A self-educated man and a pioneer farmer all his life, who had his full share in the struggles of trail-breaking, besides supporting a large family, Stephansson, nevertheless, succeeded in becoming one of the most influential and most productive Icelandic writers of his day. Six large volumes of original poems, *Andvökur*, are an eloquent testimony to his irrepressible creative urge. But great as was his productivity, the variety of his themes is equally amazing. He made up for his lack of schooling by choice, concentrated reading. As he lived always close to Mother Earth, his nature poems are rich in picturesque detail and profound thought. Nor are his many poems on themes from the sagas or other Northern lore less powerful or less poetic. A man of world-wide interest and sympathy, he frequently found inspiration in current events, always the spokesman of the suffering and the oppressed.

Cosmopolitan as Stephansson was, he was, nevertheless, Icelandic to his heart's core; and his patriotism, free from all smugness and provincialism, found expression in many noble poems.

EVENING

TRANSLATED BY JAKOBINA JOHNSON

At twilight, when I am alone with my thoughts
—The trappings of labor have shed,—
Our earth, in pursuit of its ceaseless round,
From light into shadow fled
And garrulous talk to its ultimate end
The baying of hounds has sped,

And Care on my doorstep sits drowsy at last,
Who guards all my movements by day,
Who startled my songs—all the lightest of wing—
And silent they fluttered away,
Who bruised the wing of a thought as it soared
Its heavenward call to obey.

How fain to forgive and forget would I rest,
If I—my own master once more—
Through soft-falling darkness and silence could dream
The sweet but invisible shore
That claims all our hopes which are shipwrecked in life,
And longings, which poets adore.

Where wealth that is gathered by taxes or tolls
Or tariffs—is counted as vain,
Where no man's success is another man's loss,
Nor power the goal and the gain,
The first of commandments is justice to all,
And victory causes no pain.

Then looms up before me, all ghastly and pale,
A night-time of sleepless unrest.
And I am surrounded by specters of souls
Who failed to live up to their best,
And hark to the cry of the foundlings of life:
Abilities shunned and represt.

And then I see men in a woeful abyss
Whom toil has forced to their knees,
But indolent greed on their helplessness thrives,
—Disease at the heart of our trees—
And masses bereft of their reason and will
Are baited and governed by these—

With dealings and friendships as doubtful as those
Awaiting the wanderer slow
Whom night overtakes as he sees in dismay
A bandits' encampment below,
And hears through the darkness, while feigning to sleep,
The stealthy approach of the foe.

The night of our wand'rings seems woefully long,
The wayfarers lost as of yore,
Our dawn of advancement a boastful romance,
The shadows as dense as before.
The minds of the ancients soared equally high,
Where, then, is our wonderful score?

In this—that the dawn reaches numbers increased
Through centuries slipping away.

Not higher—nor deeper—but *farther* it seeks
Like shafts of the lengthening day.
One brief wingéd moments each lifetime departs,
And sees but the tragic delay.

For even the shepherds on moorlands afar
Have felt this benevolent ray
Of slow-creeping dawn, as it touches their hearts,
Transforming their arduous day
And mine—this unquenchable longing to sing
Which sleepless at night I obey,

Till finally called—and shall calmly retire
Where sleeplessness may not assail,
Assured that whatever of good I conceived
Continues, and never shall fail.
The best that was in me forever shall live,
The sun over darkness prevail.

AT CLOSE OF DAY

TRANSLATED BY JAKOBINA JOHNSON

WHEN sunny hills are draped in velvet shadows
By summer night
And Lady Moon hangs out among the tree tops
Her crescent bright;
And when the welcome evening breeze is cooling
My fevered brow
And all who toil rejoice that blessed night time
Approaches now—

When out among the herds the bells are tinkling,
Now clear, now faint,
And in the woods a lonely bird is voicing
His evening plaint;
And when the breeze with drowsy accent whispers
Its melody,
And from the brook the joyous cries of children
Are borne to me;

When fields of grain have caught a gleam of moon-
light
But dark the ground—
A pearl-gray mist has filled to over-flowing
The dells around;
Some golden stars are peeping forth to brighten
The eastern wood;—
Then I am resting out upon my doorstep,
In nature's mood.

My heart reflects the rest and sweet rejoicing
Around, above;
And beauty is the universal language
And peace and love;
And all things seem to join in benediction
And prayers for me;
And at Night's loving heart, both earth and heaven
At rest I see.

And when the last of all my days is over—
The last page turned—
And whatsoever shall be deemed in wages

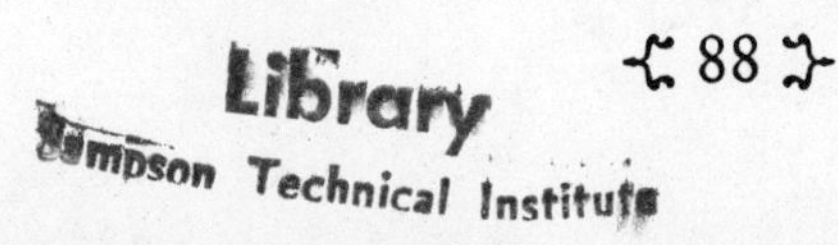

That I have earned:—
In such a mood I hope to be composing
My sweetest lay;
And then—extend my hand to all the world
And pass away.

Einar Hjörleifsson Kvaran

When the cultural history of Iceland for the last fifty years is written, it will be seen that Einar Hjörleifsson Kvaran (1859–1938) played a more important rôle in the literary and intellectual life of his nation during that period than almost any one of his contemporaries. During his ten years' residence in Winnipeg, Manitoba (1885–1895), the greater part of the time as editor of the Icelandic weekly *Lögberg*, he also made a notable contribution to the cultural life of the Icelanders in America. Upon his return to Iceland, he was for years associated in an editorial capacity with various Icelandic publications. From 1906 on he devoted himself mostly to creative literary work.

One of the most significant writers of present-day Iceland, a charming essayist, no less than a gifted journalist and a brilliant writer of fiction, Kvaran was as productive as he was versatile, and enjoyed nation-wide popularity. He was also a fine lyric poet and a dramatist of note, but his greatest contribution is in the realm of fiction. He has published four collections of short stories, many of which are veritable masterpieces of finished art. With one flash of insight he can illumine a whole life destiny.

His novels deal generally with life in Reykjavík, the capital of Iceland, during the first two decades of the present century. They are graphic and truthful pictures and at the same time profound psychological studies. Kvaran began as a realist, but in his mature works the emphasis is always on spiritual values.

MY COUNTRY LIES WOUNDED

(*From the play "Governor Lenhard"*)

TRANSLATED BY JAKOBINA JOHNSON

My bird has a note of joy today.
A brisk wind scatters the clouds in play
And tosses and tears unheeding.
But—my country lies wounded and bleeding.

My mountains loom in the distance blue,
And smile in the sunlight's golden hue,
Eternal repose conceding.
But—my country lies wounded and bleeding.

My trees seem to guard some secret dark—
The leaves seem to whisper "Hush" an[d]
"Hark,"
And move me to tearful pleading,
For—my country lies wounded and bleeding.

My fondest love is my native land.
In youth she has fired my ambitions grand,
In manhood all others leading.
And now she lies wounded and bleeding.

Oh, save her, Lord, in her tragic plight!
Reveal in a flash of holy light
These turbulent waves receding!
For, oh, she lies wounded and bleeding.

DEATH COMES RIDING

(*From the play "Governor Lenhard"*)

TRANSLATED BY JAKOBINA JOHNSON

DEATH comes riding, the road is clear.
Your loved one shall rue the meeting.
His menacing pace brings waves of fear,
As wildly he rides down the roadway clear.
Oh, heard you the hoof beats fleeting?

Death rides over the drifted snow.
The skeleton nods a greeting.
Beware, oh, beware of him, child of woe,
As wildly he rides o'er the drifted snow.
Now hear I the hoof beats fleeting.

THE ORPHAN

(*Vistaskifti*)

TRANSLATED BY MEKKIN SVEINSON PERKINS

I

THE latter half of the first decade of my life was spent at Skard. Before I was five the sea took my father from me and left me no alternative but to become a public charge.

One day, when I had been at Skard four years and three or four months, I was out in front of the house pounding fish. I wished the Lord would in some way make the sledge half as heavy and the block where I pounded it half as high, and indeed that He would make the world somehow different.

The fish that I was beating was a fine frozen fish, easily torn to shreds. I looked at every bit broken off by the blows with mingled joy and dismay. I myself would most likely take a beating for every one of them.

"Yet into my mouth they shall go," said I to myself.

I looked towards the door of the house to make sure that no one saw me. Then I slipped the flakes into my mouth.

Beyond the homefield the land in front of the house fell away to a plain, and glancing in that direction, my eye caught the figure of a horseman. It must be Jon coming home, for I made out the skewbald horse as Bleikskjoni. I could tell by the way he threw back his head, and cantered, and then galloped like a bird in flight.

I was troubled. Poor Jon! Soon he would pull up and jump down at the door of the house that he shared with Thorgerdur.

I would never come home to Thorgerdur if I were a man and master and her husband. Not I! I would always be off and away on the skewbald horse. And I wouldn't tell her where I was. She should never find me!

The thought nerved my arm and I beat with a kind of passion, even though I could still feel the ache in my shoulders and back.

The next time I looked across the homefield, I could see that Jon was reeling somewhat on the horse. He would veer to the left, then he would veer to the right, and Bleikskjoni veered, too, as he always would when his master was in this condition.

I was cheered by the observation. I knew all about this reeling and veering on the part of Jon and Bleikskjoni. When Jon was drunk, he was always good to me, but nasty to Thorgerdur. Sober, he was never good to anyone, but not nasty either.

Jon made the last stretch at a gallop. Bleikskjoni blew dense clouds of steam and was blanketed with sweat.

Jon dismounted. I saw he was unsteady on his feet, but pleased with himself and the world. His mouth and his eyes were alight, and even his ears were smiling.

He stood with feet wide apart, like a sailor on a heavy swell, and cocked his head on one side to stare at the fish I was beating.

I was pounding with might and main.

"Can you unsaddle Bleikskjoni, my lad?"

I let the sledge fall on the block, but gazed dubiously at the fish. Thorgerdur had forbidden me to leave off before I had finished. Now I did not know which to obey.

"Never mind the damn fish!"

"Are you cursing the food, Jon?" called Thorgerdur, coming up suddenly from behind, so that Jon and I, both of us, started. "No wonder this home is not blessed when you curse God's gifts. As well curse God Himself!"

Thorgerdur was as hot as Bleikskjoni. I could see the religious zeal pouring out of her in a thick sweat. She was always pious, and she was always perspiring. In those days I supposed perspiration to be the odor of sanctity.

Jon winced and then straightened up. Bestriding the

swell yet more firmly, he transfixed Thorgerdur with a look.

"Is God then a dried fish?" he asked gruffly.

For a moment Thorgerdur was speechless. She wiped her face with her apron and struggled to frame a reply. Meanwhile Jon was regarding her with triumphant eye.

"Yes, just keep on blaspheming," she said. "That's probably the best thing to do."

"Unsaddle Bleikskjoni, Steini, my lad," Jon said gently.

"He's to beat the fish." Thorgerdur's voice was resolute.

"He'll be killed," said Jon.

"Killed?" asked Thorgerdur. "Who? The fish?"

Jon did not deign a reply. He began to unsaddle the horse. In a rage he flung down the saddle on the walk in front of the house. Thorgerdur looked at him, taking in his staggering gait, obviously with no great sympathy.

Jon came over to the block and stood looking down at me.

"You'll be killed, my poor lad," he said next. "It will soon be the death of you."

It was not an inviting outlook. The tears started to run down my cheeks. But I beat doggedly at the fish.

"It'll be the death of him, will it?" asked Thorgerdur. "Who do you think is going to kill him?"

"You!" cried Jon.

He fairly shouted the word, and drew himself up so abruptly that he almost fell over backwards. Then he swayed towards Thorgerdur.

"That's nice talk! See if you can't stand up! Where did you call?"

"At Stadur."

"At Stadur? You didn't get liquor there—not from the minister?"

"Liquor?—There?—Didn't have to get it there, old woman. Got it from myself," said Jon.

He drew a flask out of the breast pocket of his coat, removed the cork, spat, and took a swig.

"Got something else from the minister, though—something for you."

"For me?" Thorgerdur was clearly impressed. Again Jon moved away from her, but nearer the block, and stood looking at me once more. As he stroked the dark red whiskers which encircled his jaws like a collar, he assumed a more pensive tone.

"It's not just me that's concerned for your life, you poor thing."

"Stop that confounded nonsense, Jon!" cried Thorgerdur.

She placed her arms akimbo, thrust her stomach forward and her shoulders back, her voice and also the expression in her eyes becoming more gentle.

"What did you get for me then?"

"What I told you."

Thorgerdur looked at him as a troll would look at a clear sky.

"He knows it," said Jon.

"Who knows what?"

"The minister."

"What does he know?"

"That he'll be killed."

Thorgerdur had been red in the face from the rush of

blood and the sweat. Now her face turned yet redder, but she didn't utter a word.

"He demands that Steini come to church next Sunday," said Jon.

"Who demands that?"

"The minister."

"What is that boy to do at church? What hypocrisy! What can he understand of God's word? What can he understand of the merciful dispensations God has made for the salvation of men? What do you understand of them for that matter?"

"Oh, not much." Jon spat and took another swig from the flask. "But he's going. He'll go. I've promised the minister. He'll have to!"

By this time Jon was drunk no less with courage and determination than with liquor. He snatched the sledge from my hands and began pounding the fish, saying with every violent blow:

"He shall!"

"What is he to ride on?" asked Thorgerdur, and there was yielding in her voice. "There are many going to church this next Sunday, and I don't believe there'll be any nag left for him."

"That's none of my business. He shall!" And Jon rained heavy blows on the fish.

"And what is he to wear?"

"Probably the clothes you've given him. Surely you haven't failed to make merciful dispensations?"

"Are you going to spoil the fish entirely, man?"

The bits flew in all directions, leaving only a bald area of skin.

Thorgerdur took the fish—both those that had been beaten and those that were still unbeaten—and placed them under her arm.

"Now go out and tend the sheep, Steini," she said. "And remember that if any of the ewes are missing, you get nothing to eat till you've found every one of them, if it takes you till this time next year."

She went into the house with the fish. Jon followed, holding the fish skin with what few shreds of flesh still clung to it. He was swinging the skin with such force that these fell, one by one, to the ground.

"He shall go to church," Jon muttered. "I don't suppose you'd want the minister to—"

I heard no more, for by now Jon was inside the house.

I lingered as long as I dared, picking up the morsels of fish. Then I started off slowly to herd the sheep. I thought about going to church next Sunday, and about not getting anything to eat until this time next year, and about this business of being killed.

And I cried. It was a hard lot indeed to be a pauper farmed out to Thorgerdur.

II

THE next day, which was Saturday, it became evident that Jon had prevailed. He didn't say a word to me. When sober, he was always taciturn. But Thorgerdur told me that if I could get a horse to ride and clothes to wear, I might go to church with them in the morning.

I asked who was to herd the sheep and drive them out,

for I knew that the folks always started for church at milking time and did not return until I had begun gathering my flock together again in the late afternoon.

Thorgerdur said that I, of course, would gather the flock together in the morning. She seemed to consider it beneath her to be discussing this matter with me. It was none of my business.

In her presence I felt a chill in the air. While she talked with me, I felt sure going to church wouldn't be any fun at all. But as soon as she was out of sight, my heart glowed, and I thought it would be indescribable bliss.

There would be no difficulty about getting a mount. I would go to old Thordur of Vik. Others found it hard to deal with him, it was true. Most youngsters were scared to death of him; he would get mad when one least expected it. I knew it wouldn't have been any use for Thorgerdur to ask favors of him, but I wasn't afraid of him. Once, while watching my flocks, I had caught his blazed mare just as she was about to run away up the mountain. Blesa was a fine animal, and Thordur loved her dearly. I knew he had never forgotten that. He never forgot anything. He told me at the time that if I ever needed anything, and if he could ever do me a favor, I should let him know. Still, it would be dreadful if he should get angry.

I found Thordur in the smithy. He seemed more gigantic than usual; his wolfish-gray head towered to the ceiling when he stood upright and blew the bellows, and the grime on his face had formed circles under his eyes and gave him a terrifying appearance.

He took the red-hot iron out of the fire and forged nails for horseshoes. As yet he hadn't spoken, and I didn't dare to say a word. Seating myself on the threshold of the smithy, I gaped at him in wonder and admiration. One after another, the nails fell from the anvil to the floor. I shuddered again and again at the thought that they might have struck me, glowing hot as they were. How strong his hands were, and his bare arms! If I had hands and arms like that, Thorgerdur would not order me around or beat me. She would be too scared. I looked at his face. His nose was like a mountain range, and his cheek-bones like foothills, and his eyesockets like the small caves up in the pass. Thorgerdur had told me that awful creatures lived in those caves; if I were deceitful and disobedient—as I usually was, she said—they would eat me up! No, no, Thordur was a good man, and I wasn't going to be scared. I was bound to ask him for the horse. If I only knew that it would do some good and not throw him into a rage!

Thordur now replaced the iron in the fire and blew. "What's on your mind, Steini, my boy?" he asked.

I jumped. It was time to speak out. "I'm to be allowed to go to church." I could get no further. I hardly knew what I was doing.

"Well? So you're to be allowed to go to church! Now, what do you say to that! Thorgerdur's going to see that your soul is saved after all! Maybe she'll get around to saving your body some day. But say, has the worthy woman secured a horse for you?"

"I have no horse."

"What? No horse! No, I'll wager you haven't! No horse, my poor lad! That would be too munificent! But

I'm not going to see you walk it. How about the blazed mare? No one has a better right to ride her for once in a way. She won't stagger under your weight."

From the look in his eyes at this moment I could see that he thought me no giant.

"Now, then," he went on, "of course, you have good clothes to wear? Oh, of course. A woman like that, so generous, so free-handed, wouldn't think those things you have on quite splendid enough for church, fine as they are!" He looked wryly at the great hole in the front of my jacket.

"I'd have to borrow clothes, too."

Thordur fairly whooped.

"Oh, you'd have to borrow clothes, too! O soul of goodness! What a generous thought on her part! Sent you out to borrow some clothes! Why don't you take my Siggi's clothes? They'll not be too tight, I imagine, though he is younger than you. Can't I send them over to you with the mare, early in the morning? You're expected to herd the sheep before you set out? Yes, I thought as much. You'll not have much time to run around fetching the horse and the clothes."

I got up from the threshold and held out my hand to Thordur.

"Oh, thank you," I said. I was so overcome that I dared not look up.

"It's nothing, Steini, my lad." His voice was so kind all at once that I started to cry, and I hurried out without even saying goodbye.

Thordur stuck his head out of the door and called after me:

"Remember me to the generous, the worthy, the honorable lady, and say I'm surprised her piety, for all its texture and firmness, would not stretch far enough decently to cover that small body of yours even if it was only with rags. Oh, no! You'd best not tell her that. She might beat you. Maybe I will tell her a little something myself one day. She won't amuse herself long with beating me!"

Thordur laughed.

III

I DID not sleep much that night.

To think of being dressed in nice clothes and riding the blazed mare all the way to Stadur! I could not think of anything else. Of sleep least of all. It was far to Stadur, very far. I knew that Skard was the last farm at the very edge of the parish and Stadur was close to the middle. I did not recall having heard that anyone ever went farther than to Stadur, except when rounding up the sheep from the mountain pastures. I had never done that. Only grown-up men could do that. Stadur was at the end of the world. And it must be beautiful there! Every day I could see the mountain above Stadur, a luminous blue, quite different from the color of the mountain that was above Skard.

If only Thorgerdur were not going! I couldn't remember anything that had ever been fun when she was along. I often thought it fun to go out to the meadows at haying time, when I would be sent on some errand, but the moment she steamed into sight I would know there was going to be trouble.

And yet, maybe going to church would turn out to be

lots of fun. Surely it could not fail to be fun! I would harbor no doubts about that! Lying there wide awake, I planned how I would lag behind, then overtake them at a gallop, and rush past like a streak of fire.

I tossed in my bed. It seemed to me so hard and bumpy. I had never noticed that before. And the woollen sheets were so harsh. I hadn't noticed that either. All around me the rest of the household were snoring. How could they sleep like that, unperturbed, on the eve of so great an event? And how was it that the blazed mare had become skewbald, and Bleikskjoni had turned to pure white, and Thorgerdur was a spotted cow with large horns? I was thinking such jumbled nonsense, till at last I stopped thinking entirely.

I was waked about five o'clock the next morning to go out for the sheep. It seemed I had just fallen asleep, but I rose, quickly shaking off sleep, for the weather was fine. The sun had just come up over the eastern edge of the mountains. In the valley the fog had left the visible world, all except a few wisps drifting aimlessly over the river, moving vaguely in all that bright sunlight, until they should be dissolved, and every blade of grass in the valley glittered with tears of joy.

When I reached home with the ewes, the blazed mare was standing, saddled, with the other horses in front of the house. I was told that the clothes had arrived and that I must hurry, for the folks were about to start. I have never changed clothes with more pleasure. There was everything. There was even fresh underclothing. I remember that what I prized most was a white linen shirt, to be worn outside the woollen one. I felt like a prince in all that elegant outfit. Yet I didn't dare look anyone in the face; they would think it so funny to see me in proper clothes.

We were on the way. I hung back. Then giving the horse a crack with the whip, I went flying out the home-field, and left them all far behind.

Thorgerdur called to me:

"Don't you know that you're to take off your cap and say the Lord's Prayer when you start for church? You know the Lord's Prayer, though you are a dunce. You knew that when you first came here. And then you're to pray the Lord that the service may prove a blessing to you and may lead to your soul being saved. Though I don't think there's much chance of that." Thorgerdur sighed; to her mind I was very ungodly and sinful.

But I saw all the men were bareheaded and were walking their horses slowly. Like the rest, I uncovered my head, and waited until they had put their hats on and I could let the mare gallop off again.

That I did as soon as the prayers were over. I was vibrating in every limb. The mare felt that now she could go. The hummocks along the road fairly spun past, and yet Blesa's gait was as smooth as the bed of my master and mistress. In front was the mountain above Stadur, towering to the sky and bright blue. I forgot everything except my joy—everything, even Thorgerdur.

But she called me again:

"What's got into the brat to make such an exhibition! Rushing off before all the rest like a lunatic! Are you going to break that creature's wind? Listen, Jon, he's not fit to ride that horse."

"It was lent to him," said Jon.

"You let me ride it."

Jon grunted a kind of assent.

Presently all dismounted and various changes were made. Thorgerdur's saddle was placed on the blazed mare and mine was transferred to the worst pack horse on the farm.

Now I no longer galloped ahead. I thought the old nag would cleave me in two with every step, if he were to go fast at all.

Sigga, one of the hired girls, also rode a poor horse, and we straggled far in the rear.

"Are you mad, Steini? Look at me. You aren't crying? I got a little sugar last summer in the village. I have a lump right here. There, take it, poor chap."

"I don't feel like eating it," said I.

"You must be in a fury!" said Sigga.

I whipped up the nag to get away from her and I cried unrestrainedly. I felt no less dismal than angry.

The mountain above Stadur was not blue when I reached it, nothing but black rocks and gray landslides, to me a great surprise. Nevertheless I was almost beginning to think this was fun after all.

Such a crowd at the church! I had never seen so many people. On the grassy plain between Stadur and the sea I was hemmed in by countless riders from all the farms. They were all riding fast. The younger ones were laughing, and the laughter seeped into my consciousness. I no longer cared that my nag had so rough a gait. I urged him ahead, dug my heels into him, whipped him, pulled on the reins, and shook my whole body. But I took good care not to look in the direction of the blazed mare, who ran forward as smoothly as a bird.

All the people dismounted at the public corral right below the homefield and placed their horses inside. The farmers greeted each other, blew their noses, took out their snuff horns, removed the taps from them, knocked the horns on the side with the taps, snuffed, offered one another a pinch, and remarked that the weather now wasn't bad, but it couldn't possibly last. They believed it would change that evening, they said; it was beginning to look overcast out to sea. The small boys had gathered in a crowd. First they looked at the ground solemnly and shyly; then they began to examine each others' neckpieces and buttons, and before anyone realized what was happening, they had begun pushing each other and fighting. Their mothers separated them, shook them, and said that that was nice behavior for church. The women, meanwhile, were busy removing their riding togs, shaking creases out of their skirts, and taking their shawls out of pouches and bundles. Daring young men made offers of help to the younger ones, and the girls laughed and said they had no need of help. But the young men helped them anyway.

I stood apart, gazing enraptured at all this activity.

Then Thorgerdur came to me.

"What a sight you are, boy! What have you got all over your face? Just as if you were a spotted sheep. Always the same dirty fool! Always bawling and whimpering! Now go wash your face in the brook over there."

I turned to go to the brook. Close to us was standing one of the older women, tall, thin, and pale, in a dark shawl. I felt sure she had overhead all that Thorgerdur said. She followed me to the brook and sat down on the bank.

"Do you live at Skard?" she asked.

I nodded assent.

"You are probably a foster-child?"

"No, I'm a parish boy."

"How old are you?"

She thought for a moment after I had replied to that question.

"My son Oli would be his age now, if he were alive," she said to herself.

I could not explain later how it all came about, but in a twinkling she had adroitly wormed out of me who owned the clothes I was wearing, and what had happened to Blesa, and I don't know how much more. There seemed to be so much love in her voice and the expression in her eyes was so kindly that I was as if hypnotized.

Thorgerdur came over to us. She greeted the woman effusively, hugging and kissing her many times and thanking her for past favors. She was all aflutter. The stranger was courteous, but impressed me as a bit frigid.

"So you took one of the children of the late Grimur of Grund," said the woman.

"Yes."

"He's a nice-looking boy."

"Do you think so? I want to bring him up in the fear of God and with good morals, but I'm afraid that is going to be hard."

The woman passed by that lament. The church bells

had begun to ring. She left us and went over to her husband, and together they started up the homefield towards the church.

Thorgerdur seized my arm rather roughly.

"What was Ragnhildur of Dal worming out of you?"

I was silent.

"What was Ragnhildur worming out of you?" she insisted, pinching my arm.

I was still silent.

"Will you answer me?"

She was pinching my arm so hard that I felt the tears come to my eyes. I was bound I would not answer her. She should kill me first. But then I would come back as a ghost and would strangle her.

"You're never anything but a cross to me and to everyone else!" she said. Then she dropped my arm suddenly and went on up to the church.

I was left standing there alone rubbing my eyes. I would have to wash again to clean away the fresh smears. I washed in the brook, and walked towards the church with the rest. They were already singing inside. I paused at the door, not daring to open it. Just then several men came along. I slipped into the church behind them. A poorly dressed man was sitting in the rear pew, and that seemed the right place for me.

For a time I gazed wonderingly at the minister in his vestment and at the picture of Christ above the altar. Then I saw the blazed mare pacing, with Thorgerdur on her back. In a little while I had sprung up behind Thorgerdur and pitched her from the saddle. She lay on the ground screaming at me. But Blesa bore me on and on and on.

She was no longer touching the ground, but glided through the air, still on and on and on. I had no idea where we were going. But the closing hymn woke me with a start.

IV

THE weather prophets had been right.

As we rode through the valley, a cold raw wind met us and clouds of fog rolled in over the mountain tops. They were like hosts of evil spirits overrunning the land. I shivered at the thought of herding the sheep in the pass the next morning.

My beast plodded far in the rear, but I didn't care. Sigga sometimes spoke to me, but I answered as little as possible. I was thinking about the pale woman with the lovely voice and the kind eyes. How could Thorgerdur be the most pious of all the people I knew and also the worst? And could it be true that God was good? Then why had he given me to Thorgerdur instead of to Ragnhildur?

When we reached home Thordur was waiting for us in front of the house at Skard. He was frowning ominously, but a mocking smile played on his lips. I could see he was staring at Thorgerdur and the blazed mare.

"May I help the kind lady dismount?" he asked, as Blesa drew up. He extended both arms genially, but his voice was cold.

"Thank you, my dear Thordur. Won't you come in and have a drop of coffee?" She was very sweet.

"She must be afraid of him," thought I. To tell the truth, I was almost afraid of him myself.

"Me? Coffee?" said Thordur. "No. I've plenty of coffee at home."

"To be sure," Thorgerdur replied, her voice soft as down.

The help stood stock-still in the yard, evidently expecting a scene.

"I've been wondering," said Thordur, "what was the text of the minister's sermon?"

"That's odd," remarked Thorgerdur. "I didn't suppose you gave much thought to such matters, since we never see you at church."

"Not give thought to such matters, eh? I've been thinking of them to some purpose. And I've figured it out. I'll wager this was the text, 'But from him that hath not shall be taken away even that which he hath.' How could it have been anything else?" He was looking from me to the mare.

"So that's what it is!" Thorgerdur exclaimed with a rising asperity. "You begrudge me the use of the mare because I'm a trifle heavier than that youngster there? Well, I can allow you a little something for that. But you've no business quoting and misapplying the Scriptures, you atheistical pagan!"

Snatching her saddle off the mare's back, Thordur flung it beyond the roadway.

"An atheist, am I, then, and an unbeliever? That's too bad! Anyway, I believe that those who oppress the poor are hateful in the sight of the Lord. I believe those who mistreat small children entrusted to them will be cast into the outer darkness. I believe you will go to hell, Thorgerdur! That religion is as good as another." Flinging his saddle on the mare's back, Thordur rode off on her like a tempest.

Thorgerdur, stock-still, looked after him, trembling with rage. The hired help stole off into the house, one by one. I was following suit, but Thorgerdur shouted to me. I went to her, but not too near.

"This is all your doing, you fine fellow!" she said, her voice hoarse and shaky.

She was silent for a moment. She was meditating some plan. I waited a while. I was again edging around to the door when she called me:

"Go on in and get something to eat. You're to spend the night tending the sheep in the pass. They may get lost in the fog unless someone takes care of them. And you know what you'll get, boy, if you should lose any of them!"

With that she was rid of her spite. She went in. The world turned black before me. To spend the whole night in the pass, all alone, in the darkness and fog! I had never been told to do that before; I had never supposed that it would be required of me until I was man-grown. And I couldn't imagine that I should ever be so big that I should have that much courage.

I did not cry now as I clambered up the mountainside to the sheep; I had already cried so much that no tears were left.

But when I got to the pass, and the fog closed in around me, cold and gray and dark, and the blackness of night drenched the fog as water drenches a cloth, I felt quite alone and abandoned. No man and no God. No one, only me and the trolls in the little caves in the pass. It would probably be for the best if they ate me up. But that would be so awful!

I sat down on a stone and sobbed.

V

I WAS fetching water and I felt my bare hands would drop off.

No warmth in the late winter sun. The valley was covered with snow. Away to the south, snow; up on the mountain and down by the river, snow; high snowdrifts embanked the house; a deep thatching of snow lay on the roofs, and above the banked whiteness was an atmosphere whirling with snow. At times it was borne straight ahead by the wind; then again, it was eddied about and formed a stifling cover, pressing in from every direction till one did not know which way to turn.

The cold laid an icy bridge over every streamlet. It was sucked through the passages in the house, chilling everyone to the marrow the moment a door was opened, freezing everything that was wet, tormenting man in every conceivable way and mocking him into the bargain, for it left fairy garlands of roses inscribed on the window panes. But perhaps all it wanted was to build him a fairy palace, and that was the best it could do.

I was trudging over the road with those pails when Jon came riding up on Bleikskjoni. He was back from a meeting of the farmers of the district held the day before. He and I were both covered with snow.

"Hello, Steini, my boy," said Jon, swinging down.

"Fine! He's tipsy," said I to myself.

"Take Bleikskjoni out to the stable," said Jon, "and give him a mouthful of hay. Then scrape the snow off yourself and come in by the fire."

After a while I came inside. Jon had removed his outer clothing and was sitting on his bed in his shirt sleeves. On a chair opposite the bed sat Thorgerdur, spinning. The wheel whirred at a rate even brisker than usual.

I sat down on my bed in the outer *badstofa.** The door to the bedroom of the master and mistress stood open.

Thorgerdur called to me: "Have you finished fetching the water?"

I replied that I had.

"Then go and clean out the stable. That wasn't done this morning."

"There's no hurry," said Jon.

Thorgerdur sighed her impatience.

"Very well. Have your own way."

She went at the wheel with fresh fury till it creaked and whined in every part.

"Come here, Steini, my boy, and sit by me," Jon said.

I made as if I had not heard him. I thought this too great an honor, and I didn't think it either desirable or conducive to peace for me to be in there along with the master and mistress.

"Come, Steini," said Jon again.

This time I obeyed. I sat down, and Jon patted my head.

* In an old-fashioned Icelandic farmhouse, the *badstofa,* literally bathroom, is a bedroom and sitting room combined. Here the members of the household spend their evenings spinning, sewing, reading, carding wool, and performing similar tasks.

"Now I'm drunk," said he. "I'm always kindly when I'm drunk. Then I want to have by me every creature that's suffering or oppressed."

He continued stroking my head.

"Then I realize that I'm not a bad sort. Then I want to smite evil, for I hate all tyranny, all cruelty, all brutality. That shows I am good at heart."

No answer.

"Don't you think so, Steini?" he asked me then, but his gleaming and bloodshot eyes were fixed upon Thorgerdur.

In my mind I agreed with him, but I thought it safest to say nothing.

"Drunk and noisy," said Thorgerdur, "if that's any virtue!"

Jon looked past her, out of the window. He seemed to think it beneath him to look down where Thorgerdur sat. In among the figures in the middle of the windowpanes were spots not covered with frost. Through them I saw the wind-driven snow flying past, and I heard the storm on the roof. Now a storm was brewing inside.

"Because I'm good I'm happy now," Jon said, as if speaking to someone outside the window.

"You're happy all right!" said Thorgerdur.

"I'm not happy because I'm drunk. I've another reason."

Thorgerdur continued spinning furiously. Jon still looked out of the window with a self-important and knowing look on his face. Finally he turned to me.

"Maybe you won't be killed after all," he insinuated.

It wasn't clear to me what that had to do with the matter.

But Thorgerdur gave him a look.

"What's the news from the meeting?" she asked.

"Oh, this and that," said Jon, elated, and he snuffed, taking much longer for that operation than usual.

"The paupers were up for auction," he continued, replacing the snuff horn in his trousers pocket.

I did not know what an auction was, but it began to dawn on me that something must have taken place which concerned me, and I pricked up my ears.

"Is that so? Which of them?" asked Thorgerdur.

"The worst ones."

I began to cry, for I felt sure that I belonged to that class and that insulting remarks had been made about me at the district meeting.

"And which ones are they?" inquired Thorgerdur. It was obvious she was getting extremely impatient at the difficulty of dragging the news out of him.

"The ones that are treated the worst," said Jon. "Don't cry, Steini. You'll not be killed."

This was, of course, reassuring. Yet I cried still louder.

"What are you bellowing for, Steini?" asked Thorgerdur. "You needn't be afraid you'll be put up at auction. I will never let you go. I've said that often."

Then I understood that auction had something to do with being sent somewhere else and that this could not happen to me. I continued crying.

"When did you say that?" asked Jon.

"I have said it often. Haven't I just told you that?

I suppose I'm to have my way in such a trifling matter."

Jon stood up and put his hand into the pocket of his coat, which hung over the head of the bed. Pulling out his flask, he took a deep draught, replaced the flask, and sat down on his bed.

"That's not certain," said he, in a voice that was stern, at the same time giving his wife a piercing glance.

This so startled me that I stopped crying.

"Then who's to decide it? You?" asked Thorgerdur. Respect for her husband was not plainly perceptible in her voice.

"What would you say about the local welfare board?" asked Jon. "Olafur of Gil wanted him."

"For how much?" asked Thorgerdur.

"The same price they pay you."

"They won't move him then."

"Finnur of Hol wanted him."

"For how much?"

"Ten crowns less."

"We ought to be able to do that also," said Thorgerdur.

My heart began to beat unusually fast.

"Sveinn of Borg wanted him."

"For how much?"

The spinning wheel had stopped. Leaning forward, Thorgerdur stared at Jon eagerly.

"Twenty crowns less."

So this was what they meant by an auction!

In my excitement I turned hot and cold by turns. Why didn't Jon say at once what the outcome had been? Why did he make her drag every word out of him?

"Blast him!" cried Thorgerdur. "Of course, you made

the same offer? Of course, you did. You agreed. Why on earth don't you answer me? If you didn't agree, then we'll do so now."

Thorgerdur seemed to swell with hidden excitement.

"Thorarinn of Dal wanted him," he brought out.

I knew that Thorarinn of Dal was the husband of the pale woman who had talked to me by the brook. Quite beside myself, I jumped up from the bed, walked over to Thorgerdur's spinning wheel, and leaning against it, gaped at her like an idiot. All fear of her had vanished under the effect of my excitement. And all sense, too. Nothing left but a numb consciousness that I was being battered from one side to the other; that on one side was heaven, and on the other, hell.

"For how much?" asked Thorgerdur.

I don't believe any human being ever spent so long taking snuff as Jon did at this painful crisis.

At last he spoke: "For nothing, my dear old woman. Not a single thing, not half an *eyrir*,* not one solitary sheep's dropping!"

For one moment Thorgerdur sat motionless and speechless. Then she pushed me aside and spun one skein of wool in silence and at a frantic speed. While I shrank back to the bed, Jon looked at her, grinning amiably.

She did not take another skein. She seemed quite beside herself. Winding the end of the wool about the spindle support as if in a trance, she pushed the wheel away from her.

"The sly vixen!" she said. "Isn't that just like Ragnhildur? But do you know what I'm going to do? I'll keep

* The smallest Icelandic coin, worth about one fifth of a cent.

him for nothing myself. I'll not have Ragnhildur deciding things in my home. She'll have to find some other way to amuse herself than by taking my help away from me."

Now I thought I could make out to which side I was being driven in this game of shove and push. Sigga, the hired girl, had told me that a predetermined fate, either good or bad, was allotted to everyone; some were born to be lucky and others to be unlucky. Queer justice, that! It filled me with dread. And now I knew which fate was intended for me. I was destined to be alone, helpless, and an outcast from the world all my life, and I wished that my life might be terminated that very day.

Jon emptied the flask. Then he spoke:

"Listen, Thorgerdur. Now I'm drunk, and so I'm good. I'm glad that for once you are made to realize what you really are like. But I'm not so drunk that you need question one word that I say. You would not be allowed to keep Steini even if you should offer the welfare district a thousand crowns for the privilege. Your friend Thordur told Ragnhildur how you treat the child and got her to offer to take him. Thordur says Ragnhildur suspected something after seeing Steini last summer at church. He told the chairman of the welfare board that Steini's a very good child and that you're the worst old hag on all God's green earth. And if Thordur had not spoken out, I'd have told him myself."

"You!" said Thorgerdur.

Ever since I have marvelled at the prodigious anger and contempt she contrived to pack into that one monosyllable.

"Yes, me," said Jon gruffly. "I would not have allowed you to kill the child in my home. For I have a good heart.

I'm not a bad sort. I know that now better than ever. For now I'm drunk. And I'll never let you decide anything for me—never!"

"Well, we'll talk about that tomorrow," said Thorgerdur. Plainly she did not intend he should keep the bit in his teeth, but she was so shaken for the moment by this defeat that she went to bed, pulled the covers over her head, and lay there all the evening.

This left Jon free to fill his flask again from a cask of liquor he had on hand. He became more and more incoherent as the evening wore on. Now and then he stroked my head and patted me, telling me that now he was drunk and that now he was good.

Neither Jon nor Thorgerdur ordered me to do any work, so I didn't turn a hand. I seemed to be living in a dream.

Outside the storm grew worse. The wind beat on the roof. Night dropped down upon the earth, cold and raw and dark. Every window became a sheet of ice.

But in the window panes of my future was one bright loophole. Through it I could glimpse the blue sky, in which floated air castles in wonderful, beautiful, vague, and dreamlike colors.

VI

THE last few days of winter * were unusually cold. The ground was all frozen, and a cold north wind blew. The live stock had to be stall-fed.

Out in the road, old Thordur of Vik was telling Thor-

* According to the Icelandic calendar, summer begins the last week in April.

gerdur that in two weeks' time he wouldn't have one damned mouthful of hay left if this kept on, and everything would perish—sheep, cattle, and horses—everything would go to the devil, everything one cared for.

Thorgerdur smiled, for she had plenty of hay.

"But not anything else," said Thordur when he saw the smile. "So there's no danger that you will go there too. That's the way things are in this world. And now may God be with you!" Pricking the hard frozen ground with his alpenstock, he went off.

Thorgerdur didn't answer him, but turning to me she said: "Shame on you! Now go on in and get the water pails."

Thordur did not come to the end of his hay supply after all. A few days later came a change for the better. First, a gentle southerly breeze; then I became aware of the smell of earth from the walls of the house, and to me it was a delightful fragrance. The snowy blanket gradually darkened and sank. The ground began to turn brown in spots, and the patches increased. There were bound to be floods. Crouchmas was at hand.

And there were indeed floods. Everything that had been cold and solid was now melted and set in motion. The southerly breeze gathered strength. Water formed wherever one pressed a foot, wherever one looked, wherever one listened—singing water. The snowdrifts up on the mountainsides turned into streams, rushing head over heels. The ice in the hollows formed restless pools, tiny lakes that sparkled as though with the thought of plunging off and away on a dance to the sea. But they found no escape except into the air, and that took such a long time.

"Suppose you can't get to Dal on Crouchmas Day?" asked Sigga.

"Get to Dal?"

"Yes, on account of the floods. Who's to get you over the rivers?"

"Then I'll go when I can," said I.

But that was only bravado. It seemed to me that if I couldn't get away on Crouchmas Day, I could not go on living.

"But suppose you eat yourself into the service again?" asked Sigga.

My bewilderment must have shown in my face like one big question mark.

"Don't you know that if you eat dinner in the old place on Crouchmas Day you are bound there for the next year?"

"Then I won't eat," said I.

I thought about that all day long until I went to sleep that night, and again when I woke the next morning, how terrible it would be if I couldn't get away, and how I wouldn't eat a bite, and how dreadfully hungry I'd be if I didn't have anything to eat maybe for a whole week.

I couldn't contain myself for impatience. I doubted that I really could get away, and it seemed to me that the time would never pass. I imagined what great joy it would be to go, especially on horseback, to ride away and know that I never had to return to Skard. But then my mind became filled with doubts again.

Crouchmas Day dawned bright and clear. I woke up very early, at dawn, in the brightness of the spring. Having heard plans made the night before, I knew that I was to go that day and that Thorgerdur herself was to take me. There had been a frost for several nights and only slight thaws in the daytime, so that the waters had sunk in streams and rivers. There was nothing to prevent me from travelling over the district. Yet I was afraid something might happen to prevent me from starting. I waited for the others to wake up, staring first at the window, then at my bedpost, and then at my hands. How could they go on sleeping so soundly!

"What is he to wear?" asked Thorgerdur, as the time for the journey approached.

"I don't know, my love," said Jon. "Isn't he to wear his own clothes? And wouldn't it be best to hurry and saddle the horses?"

His voice was gentle. I realized that Jon was eager we should start as soon as possible and that there should be no scene.

"Do you think I'll take the brat in these rags? Do you think I'll ride through the valley with him in such tatters?"

"No," said Jon, still more humbly. "Of course not! Last summer old Thordur lent him . . ."

"And it's your idea—?" Thorgerdur brushed aside that suggestion. "He'll have to wear little Jonas's Sunday suit. Only it will get all dirty and wrinkled!"

So I was dressed in the best clothes of her son Jonas, and I was told to go and say goodbye.

I ran here and there to find the members of the household—in the house and out on the homefield—and I kissed them all. I was beside myself with joy.

I found Jon out in the shed.

"Goodbye, Steini, my boy," said he. Taking a crown

out of his purse, he stuck it into my vest pocket. "Remember to take this out of your pocket when you take the clothes off, and don't let Thorgerdur see it."

I gave him an extra kiss for the crown.

By the time we set out I was worn out with joy at actually having started and at the thought of the crown. I began to love all the people to whom I had said good-bye, Jon most of all. Even Thorgerdur wasn't so bad, after all. But I could hardly formulate a clear thought. I was in a kind of happy daze. Luckily, Thorgerdur hardly spoke to me the whole way.

Ragnhildur was out in front of the house when we arrived. I jumped off the horse at once.

Ragnhildur turned to me:

"Well, here you are, Steini, my child. You are welcome indeed. How do you do? What lovely clothes you're wearing! Isn't that fine?" The same kindness in her voice and the same gentleness in her eyes as last summer at the church.

Yes, this was fine, even if the clothes were not mine.

"God bless you, and how are you, my dear Ragnhildur," said Thorgerdur. "Here I've brought the dear boy. I'm afraid I'll have to ask you to help me dismount."

Ragnhildur complied with that request. Then Thorgerdur gave her two kisses, and added a third before she let her out of her embrace.

"Yes, here I've brought him, the poor dear boy. I think I'll miss him in my home. I would hate parting with him to anyone except you. Though he has many faults, he's a very obedient child, and I've done my poor best to bring out the good in him. I don't have much fear for him in a home like yours, but I'd have taken it hard to have turned him over to certain people I know."

"Won't you please come in?" asked Ragnhildur.

"Bring the bundle with your clothes, Steini, my boy," said Thorgerdur.

I unfastened the saddle bag, in which my clothes had been packed, and slung it over my shoulder.

Then we went into the bedroom of the master and mistress of the house, beyond the *badstofa.* Ragnhildur asked us to be seated on the beds.

"Won't you stay here with us tonight, Thorgerdur? It will soon be dark," she said.

"No, thank you, my dear. I promised my friend, Jorun of Hlid, to spend a night with her if I passed this way. I'm going as far as her place, so I can stay only a moment."

"Then I'll make a cup of coffee right away. The water's boiling in the kettle."

Ragnhildur went out, leaving Thorgerdur and me alone together.

"Now you better change your clothes, Steini," said Thorgerdur. "I'm going to put Jonas's clothes in the bag."

I began opening the bag and pulled my rags out of it, one by one.

"How awfully long it takes you, you rascal!" said Thorgerdur. She seemed ill at ease.

So I hurried, and after emptying the bag, I took off my coat. Then I unbuttoned my vest. At that instant I remembered the crown.

I didn't know what in the world I should do, for Thorgerdur was staring at me. No chance to get the crown without her seeing. I took off my vest and laid it on top of the coat. In my embarrassment, I took my time for all this, although Thorgerdur kept her eyes constantly fixed on me.

Just then Ragnhildur returned with coffee and pancakes.

"How quick you were, my dear," said Thorgerdur.

"What's the matter, Steini? Are you going to bed?" asked Ragnhildur, looking at me.

"Oh, no, he's just changing his clothes," said Thorgerdur in honeyed tones, although with some hesitation.

"But why? You may wear those clothes until tonight. You won't be asked to do any work today."

"The clothes are not his," said Thorgerdur, her tone still amiable.

"Whose are they, then?"

"They belong to my son Jonas."

"But where are Steini's clothes?"

"There on the bed," said Thorgerdur, pointing at the heap.

Making a wry face, Ragnhildur picked up and examined each garment.

"Are they all there?"

"Yes," said Thorgerdur. The gentleness was disappearing from her voice.

"Put the vest and coat on again, my lad," said Ragnhildur very calmly.

"My Jonas's clothes!" exclaimed Thorgerdur. I couldn't tell whether she was more astonished or angry.

"The Sunday clothes of little Steini himself," said Ragnhildur. In an instant she had slipped my coat and vest on again before Thorgerdur realized what had happened.

"Surely you're not going to—going to steal my child's clothes?" Thorgerdur choked in her excitement.

"If this be theft, go and tell it to the district judge. But I will not receive the child naked like this. And I'll keep these rags as an exhibit, to show if need be. But now do come or the coffee will get cold."

"I will not drink coffee with thieves and robbers," said Thorgerdur, and she took up her whip and rushed out.

So I was left standing there alone, stupefied, my hand on the crown in my vest pocket. I have never learned, to this day, what else may have taken place between the two women.

The change had at least been accomplished. I was at last in the home of the woman who kept me from becoming a starveling, the fate of so many orphans.

A DRY SPELL

TRANSLATED BY JAKOBINA JOHNSON

It had rained for a fortnight—not heavily all the time, but a fog had sullenly hung about the mountain tops, clinging to the atmosphere and rendering the whole of existence a dull gray color. Every little while it would discharge a fine drizzle of rain or a heavy shower down upon the hay and everything else on earth, so that only the stones would occasionally be dry—but the grass never.

We were tired of the store—indeed I should like to know who would have enjoyed it. It dated back to the beginning of last century, a tarred, coal-black, ramshackle hut. The windows were low and small, the windowpanes diminutive. The ceiling was low. Everything was arranged in such a way as to exclude the possibility of lofty flights of thought or vision.

Just now not a living soul looked in—not even those thriftless fellows who lived by chance jobs in the village and met in daily conclave at the store. We had often cursed their lengthy visits, but now that they had hired out during the haymaking, we suddenly realized that they had often been entertaining. They had made many amusing remarks and brought us news of the neighborhood. And now we cursed them for their absence.

We sat there and smoked, staring vacantly at the half-empty shelves, and all but shivering in the damp room. There was no heater in the store at any season, and the one in the office, if used, emitted spurts of smoke through every aperture except the chimney. It had not been cleaned since sometime during the winter, and we were not ambitious enough for such an undertaking in the middle of the summer.

We tried to transfer our thoughts from the store to the world outside. We made clever comments to the effect that the farmers were now getting plenty of moisture for the hay-fields, and that it would be a pity if rain should set in now, right at the beginning of the haying season. We had nothing further to say on the subject, but this we repeated from day to day. In short, we were depressed and at outs with things in general. Until the dry spell.

One morning, about nine o'clock, the bank of fog began to move. First there appeared an opening about the size of your hand, and through it the eastern sky showed a bright blue. Then another opening, and through it shone the sun.

We knew what this was called, and we said to each other: "Merely a 'morning promise' "—implying, nothing reliable. But it was more. The fog began to show thinner and move faster along the mountain ridge opposite. Then it gathered in a deep pass and lay there heaped up like newly carded, snowy wool. On either side, the mountains loomed a lovely blue, and in their triumph ignored the fog almost completely. When we ventured a look through the doorway of the store, there was nothing to be seen overhead save the clear, blue sky and the sunshine.

On the opposite shore of the fjord the people looked to us like the cairns out on the moorlands, only these tiny cairns moved in single file about the hay-fields. I seemed to smell the sweet hay in the homefields, but of course this was only my imagination. I also fancied I could hear the maids laughing, especially one of them. I would willingly have sacrificed a good deal to be over there helping her dry the hay. But of this subject no more; I did not intend to write a love story—at least, not in the ordinary sense of the word.

The dry spell lasted. We, the clerks, took turns at staying out of doors as much as possible, and "drinking deeply of the golden fount of sunshine."

In the afternoon of the third day, I dropped in at the doctor's. I felt somewhat weary with walking—and idleness—and looked forward to the doctor's couch and conversation.

"A cigar?" asked the doctor.

"Yes, a cigar," I told him. "I have smoked only six today."

"Beer or whiskey and water?" queried the doctor.

"A small drink of whiskey," I replied.

I lit my cigar, inhaling deeply of its fragrance in so doing—then exhaling through mouth and nostrils. I sighed with contentment; the cigar was excellent.

Then we began to drink the whiskey and water at our leisure. I reclined against the head of the couch, stretched out my feet, was conscious of a luxurious sensation—and sent my thoughts for a moment across the fjord, where they preferred to remain.

The doctor was in high spirits. He talked about the Japanese and Russians, the most recently discovered rays, and the latest disclosures on how it felt to die.

My favorite pastime is to listen to others speaking. I never seem able to think of any topic worthy of conversation myself, but I am almost inclined to say that my ability to listen amounts to an art. I can remain silent with an air of absorbing interest and once in a while offer brief comment, not to set forth an opinion or display any knowledge—for I have none to spare—but merely to suggest new channels to the speaker and introduce variety, that he may not tire of hearing himself speak.

I felt extremely comfortable on the couch. I thought it particularly entertaining to hear the doctor tell how it felt to die. There is always something pleasantly exciting about death—when it is reasonably far away from you. It seemed so beautifully far away from the perfume of the tobacco-smoke, the flavor of whiskey, and the restfulness of the couch; and when my mind wandered to her across the fjord—as wander it would in spite of my studied attention—then death seemed so far off shore that I could scarcely follow the description of how it felt to others to die.

In the midst of this dreamy contentment and deluge of information from the doctor, the door was somewhat hastily thrown open. I was looking the other way and thought it must be one of the doctor's children.

But it was old man Thord from the Bend.

I knew him well. He was over fifty, tall and large-limbed, with a hoary shock of hair and a snub nose. I knew he had a host of children—I had been at his door once, and they had run, pattered, waddled, crept, and rolled through the doorway to gape at me. It had seemed as hopeless to try to count them as a large flock of sheep. I knew there was no income except what the old man and woman—and possibly the elder children—managed to earn from day to day. My employer in Copenhagen had strictly forbidden us to give credit to such—and of course he now owed us more than he would ever be able to pay.

"He does not even knock—the old ruffian," I said to myself.

From his appearance, something was wrong. His face was unnaturally purplish, his eyes strangely shiny—yet dull withal. It even seemed to me that his legs shook under him.

"Can it be that the old devil is tipsy—at the height of the haying season—and dry weather at that?" I mentally queried.

The doctor evidently could not recall who he was.

"Good-day to you, my man," he said, "and what matters have you in hand?"

"I merely came to get those four crowns."

"Which four crowns?" asked the doctor.

Thord raised his voice: "The four crowns you owe me."

It was now evident that it was difficult for him to remain standing.

I felt assured that the old rascal had been drinking like a fish. I was surprised. I had never heard he was inclined that way. He lived out there on the hillside a short distance above the village. I began to wonder where he had been able to obtain so much liquor—certainly not from us at the store.

"What is your name?" asked the doctor.

"My name? Don't you know my name? Don't you know me?—Thord—Thord of the Bend. I should best of all like to get the money at once."

"Yes, that's so—you are Thord of the Bend," said the doctor. "And you are up? But listen, my good man, I owe you nothing. You owe me a small sum—but that does not matter in the least."

"I care nothing about that, but I should best of all like to get the money at once," repeated Thord.

"May I feel your hand for a minute?" said the doctor.

Thord extended his hand, but it seemed to me that he did not know it. He looked off into space, as if thinking of other things—or rather as if he had no thoughts whatever. I saw the doctor's fingers on his wrist.

"You are a sick man," he said.

"Sick?—Yes—of course I am sick. Am I then to pay you four crowns? I haven't got them now."

"It makes no difference about those four crowns, but why did you get up like this? Have you forgotten that I ordered you to remain in bed when I saw you the other day?"

"In bed?—How the devil am I to remain in bed? Tell me that!"

"You must not get up in this condition. Why, you are delirious!"

"What a fool you are—don't you know that there is a dry spell?"

"Yes, I *am* aware of the dry spell." It was evidently not quite clear to him what that had to do with the case. "Have a chair, and we will talk it over."

"A chair? No!—Who, then, should dry the hay in the homefield? I had some of it cut when I was taken down—why do you contradict me? And the youngsters have made some attempts at it—but who is to see about drying it?—Not Gudrun—she can't do everything. The youngsters?—what do they know about drying hay?—Who, then, is to do it?—Are *you* going to do it?"

"Something will turn up for you," said the doctor, somewhat at a loss.

"Something will turn up? Nothing has ever turned up for *me*."

Cold shivers passed through me. His remark rang true: I knew that nothing had ever turned up for him. I felt faint at looking into such an abyss of hopelessness. Instantly I saw that the truth of this delirious statement concerned me more than all the wisdom of the ages.

"Do I get those four crowns you owe me?"—Thord asked. He was now trembling so that his teeth chattered.

The doctor produced four crowns from his purse and

handed them to him. Thord laid them on the table and staggered towards the door.

"You are leaving your crowns behind, man," said the doctor.

"I haven't got them now," said Thord, without looking back and still making his way towards the door. "But I'll pay them as soon as I can."

"Isn't there a vacant bed upstairs at the store?" inquired the doctor.

"Yes," I answered. "We will walk with you down to the store, Thord."

"Walk with me?—Be damned!—I am off for the hayfield."

We followed him outside and watched him start out. After a short distance he tumbled down. We got him upstairs in the store.

A few days later he could have told us, if anyone had been able to communicate with him, whether they are right or wrong, those latest theories on how it feels to die.

—But who dries the hay in his homefield now?

Thorsteinn Erlingsson

THORSTEINN ERLINGSSON (1858–1914) spent some years in study at the University of Copenhagen, where he embraced the Realism of Georg Brandes and his school in literature and became a Socialist in politics. After leaving the University without taking a degree, he embarked upon a literary career in Iceland (1895) and was for several years engaged in journalism. Later he made his home in Reykjavík and earned his living by tutoring. His writings, especially his poems, soon attracted attention.

A radical in religion as well as in politics, he fiercely denounced religious bigotry and social injustice. In many of his poems he expressed his views fervently and eloquently. He had the tenderest sympathy for all living things, especially for the weak and the suffering. He also wrote exquisite patriotic lyrics and nature poems. He was a master craftsman, and one of his favorite verse forms was the Icelandic quatrain, which he used with rare success, carrying on admirably the tradition of the older masters in that field, Sigurdur Breidfjörd and Páll Ólafsson. Through his social and political views, and no less because of his lyric art, Erlingsson has had wide influence. His major single work is the narrative poem *Eidurinn* (The Oath, 1913), a series of songs on a tragic love theme, combining lyric beauty with social satire, and definitely Byronic in spirit; unfortunately, only the first part of this notable work was completed.

THE TERMS

TRANSLATED BY JAKOBINA JOHNSON

IF seeing all the fiends rebel
won't smite you with fear,
And every dignitary crushed
tradition holds dear;
And every pillar of the heavens
cloven in two;
—Then I shall calmly sing my song
while sitting with you.

And if you hate the tyrant
who would shackle your feet
And all your homage claims to make
his victory complete,
While buying praise from cringing slaves
who fawn at his shoe,
—Then I shall proudly join in that
hatred with you.

And if you love the prisoner
whose courage remains,
Who will not kneel and kiss the hand
that placed him in chains,
But dauntless, till the final judgment
carries them through,
—Sincerely, with my heart and soul,
I'll love him with you.

And if you wish the secret lore
of nature to read,

Approaching it in meekness
like a child in its need,
Accepting nothing twisted
through another man's view,
—Then humbly I'll begin at the beginning
with you.

And if you dare to sail midst crushing
ice-floes at play
—With no eternal safety bonds
insuring your day—
But speed the vessel bravely
with these perils in view,
—Then gladly all the Seven Seas
I'll voyage with you.

And when the final night of nights descends
on the shore,
And inky waves envelop us,
and land is no more—
If, when we drift, you grasp the helm,
with firm hand and true,
Content, upon that unknown deep,
I'll venture with you.

THE SNOW-BUNTING

TRANSLATED BY RUNÓLFUR FJELDSTED

HER voice was so charming, so heart-felt and clear,
That rose, from the little copse, thrilling and ringing,
Her notes were of things most beloved and dear:

A sunburst of song through the night shadows flinging.
And sweet every eve were her love lays to hear.
O, if you could guess at the wealth of her singing.

Her lays were of peace in her mountain-dale home,
Its manifold beauty in summertime gleaming;
How radiant June in the dells loves to roam;
How sorrows of winter are lost in her beaming.
How wonderful then, in the isle o'er the foam,
Of hope and of love to be singing and dreaming.

She sang, in her softest and mellowest air,
The peace undisturbed of the croft that lay nether;
Her heathery slope and her bower so fair,
Though humble and commonplace were both together;
A charm kindles all, and they seem rich and rare,
When low pipes the snowbird in balmy spring weather.

She sang in the stillness the lover's fond lay,
Of heath-moors and prospect so glorious ever;
Of infancy's happiest, tenderest day,
That prays to the summer to bide there forever;
There evenings in listening silence must stay.
There loiter the nights, nor thy dream-bond dissever.

Dear songster, thy notes are afar off from me,
Thy friend's brightest summers have all now departed;
So often he longs for his homeland and thee.
He yearns for the spring and thy lays music-hearted.
He loves in the forest his mountain-heaths free,
And nightingale's charm not the least so has smarted.

Hannes Hafstein

HANNES HAFSTEIN (1861–1922) combined the statesman and the skald according to the best fashion of his countrymen in ancient as well as more recent days. Of an excellent family on both sides, he graduated in law from the University of Copenhagen in 1886. He soon rose to a place of leadership, held many public offices, and was for a number of years a member of the Icelandic Althing. He was the first Icelander to serve as Prime Minister of his native land (1904–1909 and 1912–1914). It was an era marked by many-sided material progress. His great ability and magnetic personality won him stanch followers and admirers throughout the nation.

This popularity was greatly enhanced by his poetry, most of which is the product of his earlier years, and readily made him a general favorite with the Icelandic reading public. He was one of the pioneers of Realism in Icelandic literature, but the national note became increasingly important in his works. Vigor, freshness, and youthful ardor are his outstanding qualities. His descriptive poems are both vivid and powerful. His spiritual exhortations, patriotic poems, and love songs are of a lasting merit. His elegiac pieces, such as the touching poems in memory of his wife, are both noble in spirit and deeply felt.

SPRING

TRANSLATED BY JAKOBINA JOHNSON

THE woods have wakened, birch and oak are gay,
The warbling birds have sought the bowers.

And zephyrs fondle tenderly in play
  The leaves and flowers.

I would that I could move thee, forest fair,
  To mountainside and dale and lea.
I'd clothe those homeland places bleak and bare
  But dear to me.

I would I were an ocean current grand
  And warm as beats my pulse in spring.
I'd circle round thy shores, dear fatherland,
  And blessings bring.

O, could I, like a balmy wind convey
  The breath of spring from fell to sound.
All snows should then forever melt away
  And flowers abound.

NEARING COLD-DALE

TRANSLATED BY JAKOBINA JOHNSON

I WISH for rain—and I wish for snow,
As on through Cold-Dale our horses glide;
And that a bracing wind may blow
Down from the glacial mountainside.

We need the air, and we need the bath,
To cleanse our spirits of slothful rest.
We need the lash of an ice wind's wrath
Of manly courage a fitting test.

We need a ride where the wild winds wake
And the rain beats down in relentless mood,
That they may humbly shiver and shake
Who shiver must. It may do them good.

When a noble storm meets a manly man
—The face must tingle and foot must tire—
It draws on his latent strength to fan
The glowing coals of a hidden fire.

To brave the tempest with might and main
Lends steel to courage and spurs to pride.
—I hope there will be a rush of rain
Or an Iceland storm—on our Cold-Dale ride.

Einar Benediktsson

EINAR BENEDIKTSSON (1864–1940) is generally looked upon as the greatest Icelandic poet of the present day. The son of a richly endowed and influential political leader and an equally brilliant mother, he had an unusually eventful career. A lawyer by profession, he was a practising attorney, a district judge, and a journalist, besides interesting himself in various business enterprises as well as politics. His most lasting achievements are, however, in the realm of literature. He is the author of five volumes of poetry, published between 1897 and 1930, several of which have appeared in a second edition. His short stories, essays, and sketches reveal him as a master of prose as well. He was also an able translator, and rendered, among other things, Ibsen's *Peer Gynt* into Icelandic.

The variety of his themes is commensurate with the extent of his literary domain. He travelled widely, and his experiences and observations in many lands are frequently and strikingly manifested in his poetry. Therefore he has correctly been characterized as "the Viking who on his raids and expeditions in many lands has boldly captured new and grand themes to sing." (Dr. Gudmundur Finnbogason.) He was, nevertheless, profoundly national in the best sense of the word, and delighted in writing on Icelandic themes. He has pictured the impressive Icelandic scenery in its varied seasonal garbs and has portrayed Icelandic cultural leaders down through the years. His love for Iceland and his faith in the future and the mission of his nation is written large everywhere in his poetry.

NORTHERN LIGHTS

TRANSLATED BY JAKOBINA JOHNSON

WAS ever such vision to mortals sent
As Northern Lights in the heavens flaming?
The shoreline a golden archway framing.
—Who now is at drinking and cards content?—
The earth lies serene and on sleep intent
Under a cover of roses decaying.
Rare colors the grains of sand present.
Where waters meet, there is a silver spraying.
The north is aglow with an ornate show.
Of Borealis' displaying.

From the seventh heav'n to the ocean's rim,
The suns hold a dance with the curtain lifted.
And white-capped billows of light are shifted,
Then break on a strand of shadows dim.
An unseen hand directs at its whim
This glittering round of streamers flowing.
To regions of light from the darkness grim,
All earth-life now turns with fervor growing.
—And a crystal gaze on the glowing haze
The hoary cliffs bestowing.

How base seem the issues and trifling the call
That claims our life—or we strive denying.
Let mortals attack me with hatred defying,
I now feel at peace with each creature small.
So fair and immense is this vault over all—

And smiling the stars, though our hopes be arrested.
The mind goes soaring, no heights appall—
Divine is the power through the dust manifested.
We fathom our strength—our rights are at length
In the kingdom of light attested.

How mighty an ocean the heavens bright—
And brave the vessels attempting the sailing.
A haven they seek with courage unfailing,
Whether they swerve or their course holds right;
But none have beheld Him who gave us sight,
Nor shown us the source of these marvels abiding.
At the door of His temple, this glorious night,
In homage they pray from their hearts confiding.
But vainly they wait—for locked is each gate,
And silent the spirit presiding.

RAIN

TRANSLATED BY WATSON KIRKCONNELL

WHO knows, when raindrops are descending,
Which thirsty seed will highest grow?
Who knows, when Sabbath knees are bending,
Where God will greatest grace bestow?

Since it shall rain alike on all—
On ploughland as on stony ground—
Shall any tear unnoticed fall?
Shall any lost sheep not be found?

Who knows what status God has given—
Who here on earth is small, who great?
Each grass-blade feels the growth of heaven,
Each raindrop shares the ocean's fate.

Thorsteinn Gíslason

THORSTEINN GÍSLASON (1867–1938) came of a good family and was, on his mother's side, a direct descendant of Stefán Ólafsson, the leading secular poet of seventeenth century Iceland. He studied Scandinavian (Icelandic) philology and literature at the University of Copenhagen for several years, but upon returning to Iceland, he became successively the editor of various Icelandic papers and periodicals and took a prominent part in the struggle for the independence of his country. At the time of his death, he had for years been recognized and highly respected as the dean of Icelandic journalists. He was a versatile and prolific writer, an essayist and a lyric poet as well as a journalist, and a notable translator of both prose and verse. He likewise rendered Icelandic literature and the cultural life of the nation great service by publishing many of the works of the leading Icelandic writers of the day.

Gíslason excelled in occasional poems, and many of his memorial poems are exceptionally well done. His descriptive and nature poems are noteworthy, but his purest poetry is found in some of his simple lyrics. His prose translations include Björnson's *Arne* and Scott's *Ivanhoe;* his verse translations, major poems by Ibsen, Björnson, Fröding, and Shelley, and a number of lesser poets.

THORVALDUR THORODDSEN

TRANSLATED BY JAKOBINA JOHNSON

OVER lava beds,
Sandy barrens
And glaciers vast
The trail has led him.
Hidden treasures
Of precious knowledge
Sought in the wastes
Of his native land.

Young was he
When the way he chose
Which none had known
And none had travelled;
There read the hidden
And mystic runes,
Kept by the trolls
Through countless ages,

There from giants
In giant halls
And fairy folk
In peaks and passes,
And the guardians
Of hidden fires,
Learned of his country's
Past and present.

From the mountain-peaks
His eagle eye
Scanned his country's
Open pages.
Either glacial
Or fiery fingers
Inscribed on rocks
A wondrous story.

None before him
Read so wisely
The secret lore
Of land and people.
No one thus
Intently hearkened
To the beating heart
Of Hecla's country.

None before him
So construed
The trend in thought
Of times departed.
And to no one
Had his country
Thus laid bare
Its inmost soul.

For the unknown tongue
Of unseen patrons
And the fairy-tongue
Of founts and rivers

And the dwarf-tongue
In dark cliffs spoken—
All these he learned
And aptly wrote.

In the valleys
Along our coast-line
Lies merely half
Our world of story.
The other half
Is seen only
From the airy haunts
Of hawk and eagle.

Hence his full
And first-hand knowledge
And the wise thoughts
Of his writings.
While his native land
Is known in story
Shall his honored name
And works endure.

SPRING

TRANSLATED BY SKULI JOHNSON

The air is filled with sunlight,
With azure hue it glows;
The springtide fair the fell-tops
Touches with her toes.

The day is drawn out longer,
Deep ocean night immures;
Sandpipers soon will sing on
The hillsides and the moors.

Gudmundur Fridjónsson

GUDMUNDUR FRIDJÓNSSON (1869–   ) is one of the remarkable farmer-poets in Thingeyjarsýsla in northeastern Iceland. He has not only managed to live on a high plane intellectually, but has greatly enriched the cultural life of his community and the nation as a whole, and has won for himself a well deserved place among the foremost Icelandic writers of the day. This achievement is all the more remarkable when it is kept in mind that he is largely a self-educated man, struggling to earn a living for a large family. Moreover, his writings were for years the subject of unfair and unkind criticism, but he carried on his literary work unflinchingly, and emerged victorious.

He has come to be known as the Nestor of the older generation of present-day Icelandic lyric poets, particularly because of his fine memorial poems. He has also written a number of essays and newspaper articles, several volumes of short stories, and one novel. Having lived all his life close to the soil, he interprets Icelandic country life with minute knowledge. His short stories—and that is equally true of many of his poems—are rich in local color and in full-length portraits of the rugged and solid farm-folk of Iceland. These hard-working common people are his people; he admires and extols the old and proven virtues, but dislikes the superficialities of city life, and is hostile to newfangled ideas generally.

"WHAT LACK WE?"

(*The question was put by an Icelandic periodical*)

TRANSLATED AND ABRIDGED BY JAKOBINA JOHNSON

AN early fire
And ever-burning
On the hearth of home,
A rousing fire
That ruling minds
May shed the withes of sleep.

Faith to move mountains
And all obstructions
From the road of progress,
And welcome the silver
Found at sundown,
As well as the morning's gold.

Our spirit knows not
Youthful ways,
Nor festive bridal raiment.
Desire for light
Is dominated
By worldly needs and cares.

On our voyage
Every helmsman
Needs a guiding star;
And the mariners
—Oft divided—
Need a compass true.

Our joy of life
Lacks free expression—
Fettered by forces dark
Led by a proud king
And cold-hearted:
The vogue of any age.

All our leaders,
And rank and file,
Lack the flaming torch
Of a direct
And daring purpose
Held by the king of the Cross.

Beacons we lack,
Ever watchful
And ever burning bright,
From which the nation
May derive
Courage in times of peril.

Leads a lone path
To levels high
Affording spacious vision;
Seen from those uplands
The evenglow
Lingers till dawn of day.

From those uplands
The eye may see

A boundless, sweeping ocean—
An ocean holding
In its bosom
Precious mother-of-pearl.

May kindly rays
From heaven illumine
Lonely path and highway,
And minds responsive
Find the starry dome
A mighty source of strength.

THE OLD HAY

TRANSLATED BY MEKKIN SVEINSON PERKINS

DURING the latter part of the reign of King Christian the Ninth, there lived at Holl in the Tunga District a farmer named Brandur. By the time the events narrated here transpired, Brandur had grown prosperous and very old —old in years and old in ways. The neighbors thought he must have money hidden away somewhere. But no one knew anything definitely, for Brandur had always been reserved and uncommunicative, and permitted no prying in his house or on his possessions. There was, however, one thing every settler in those parts knew: Brandur had accumulated large stores of various kinds. Anyone passing along the highway could see that.

Brandur usually had some hay remaining in lofts and yards when spring came, and besides there was the immense stack that stood on a knoll out in the homefield be-

.ore the house. It had been there for many years and was well protected against wind and weather by a covering of sod. Brandur had replenished the hay, a little at a time, by using up that from one end only and filling in with fresh hay the following summer.

Brandur was hospitable to such guests as had business with him, and refused to accept payment for food or lodging; but very few people ever came to see him, and these were mostly old friends with whom he had financial dealings. Brandur was willing to make loans against promissory notes and the payment of interest. There were not many to whom he would entrust his money, however, and he never lost a penny. Whenever these callers came, he would bring out the brandy bottle.

The buildings at Holl were all in a tumbledown state; the furniture was no better. There wasn't a chair in the whole house; even the *badstofa* had only a dirt floor, and it was entirely unsheathed on the inside except for a few planks nailed on the wall from the bed up as far as the rafters. The clock was the sole manufactured article in the room. But friends of the old man knew that underneath his bed he kept a fairly large carved wooden chest, bearing the inscription *anno 1670*. The chest was heavy and was always kept locked. Only the nearest of kin had ever seen its contents.

Brandur was not considered obliging; it was very difficult to get to see him. Yet he was willing to sell food at any time for cash; hay, too, as long as there was still some remaining in his lofts. He would also sell hay against promises of lambs, especially wethers, once it was certain that the cold of winter was past. But his old haystack he refused to touch for anyone.

In this way Brandur stumbled down the pathway of life until he lost his sight. Even then he was still sound in mind and body. While his vision remained unimpaired, it had been his habit to walk out to the old haystack every day and stroll around it slowly, examining it carefully from top to bottom and patting it with his hands. This habit he kept up as long as the weather permitted him to be outdoors, and he did not give it up even after his sight was gone. He would still take his daily walk out to the haystack on the knoll, drag himself slowly around it, groping with his hands to feel of it, as if he wished to make sure that it still stood there, firm as a rock and untouched. He would stretch out his hands and touch its face and count the strips of turf to himself in a whisper.

Brandur still tilled the land, though he kept but little help and was living chiefly on the fruits of his former labors. He had fine winter pastures, and good meadows quite near the house from which the hay could easily be brought in. The old man steadfastly refused to adopt modern farming methods; he had never levelled off the hummocks, nor drained or irrigated the land. But he did hire a few harvest hands in the middle of the season, paying them in butter, tallow, and the flesh off sheep bellies. The wages he paid were never high, yet he always paid whatever had been agreed upon.

Old Brandur had been blessed with only one child, a daughter named Gudrun, who had married a farmer in the district. Since his daughter's marriage, Brandur kept a housekeeper and one farm hand, a young man whom Brandur had reared and who, it was rumored, was his natural son. But that has nothing to do with the story.

When Brandur had reached a ripe old age, there came a winter with much frost and snow. Time and again, some of the snow and ice would thaw, but then a hard frost would come, glazing everything in an icy coating. This went on until late in April. By that time almost every farmer in the district had used up his hay; every one of them was at the end of his store, and nowhere was there a blade of grass to feed the live stock, for the land still lay frozen under its blanket of hard-packed snow and ice. When things had come to this pass, a general district meeting was called to discuss the situation and decide what should be done. Brandur's son-in-law Jon was made chairman of the meeting.

During the discussion it was brought to light that many of the flocks would die of hunger unless "God Almighty vouchsafed a turn in the weather very soon," or Old Brandur could be induced to part with his old hay. That stack would help, if properly divided among those who were in greatest need. The quantity of hay it contained was estimated, and the general opinion expressed that if it were divided, the flocks of every farmer in the district could be fed for at least two weeks, even if they could not in that time be put out to pasture.

Jon being chairman of the District Council, as well as Brandur's son-in-law, it fell to his lot to go to the old man and ask for the hay.

So it came about that on his way home from the meeting Jon stopped at Holl. The day was cold and clear, the afternoon sun shining down upon the snow-covered landscape. The icy blanket turned back the rays of warmth as if it would have nothing to do with the sun. But wherever rocks and gravelly banks protruded, the ice appeared to be peeled off, for in those spots the sun's rays had melted it, though only at midday and on the south. All streams and waterfalls slumbered in silence under the snowy blanket. A chill silence reigned over the whole valley. Not a bird was to be seen, not even a snow bunting, only two ravens which kept flying from farmhouse to farmhouse, and even their cawing had a hungry note.

When Jon rode up to the house at Holl he found Brandur out by the haystack. The old man was carefully groping his way around the stack, feeling of it on all sides and counting the strips of turf in so loud a voice that Jon could hear him: "O-n-e, t-w-o, three."

Jon dismounted and, going over to Brandur, saluted him with a kiss.

"How are you? God bless you," said Brandur. "And who may this be?"

"Jon of Bakki," replied the visitor. "Gudrun sends greetings."

"Ah, yes. And how is my Gunna? Is she well?"

"She was well when I left home this morning. Now I am on my way back from the meeting that was held to discuss the desperate situation—you must have heard about it."

"Yes, certainly, I've heard about it. I should say so! One can't get away from talk of hay shortage and hard times. That is quite true. Any other news?"

"Nothing worth mentioning," answered Jon. "Nothing but the general hard times and hay shortage. Every farmer at the end of his tether, or almost there; no one with as much as a wisp of hay to spare, and only a few likely to make out till Crouchmas without aid."

"Too bad!" said Brandur. "Too bad!" And he blew out his breath, as though suffocating from strong smoke or bad air.

For a while there was silence, as if each mistrusted the other and wondered what was in the air. Brandur stood there with one hand resting on the haystack, while he thrust the other into his trousers pocket, or underneath the flap of his trousers. He always wore the old-fashioned trousers with a flap; in fact, had never possessed any other kind. Meanwhile, holding the reins, Jon stood there gazing at the hay and making a mental estimate of it. Then he turned to his father-in-law and spoke:

"The purpose of my visit to you, my dear Brandur, is to ask that you let us have this hay—this fine old hay that you have here. The District Council will, of course, pay you; the parish will guarantee payment. We have discussed that matter fully."

When Jon ceased speaking, Brandur blew the air from his mouth in great puffs, as though deeply stabbed by a sharp pain in the heart. For a while he held his peace. Then he spoke:

"Not another word! Not another word! What's this I hear? My hay for the district? My hay to supply all the farmers in the district? Do you think for one moment that this little haystack is enough to feed all the flocks in the whole district? Do you think this tiny haycock will be enough for a whole parish? I think not!"

"But we have calculated it," protested Jon. "We have estimated that the hay in this stack will be enough to feed the flocks in the district for about two weeks, if a little grain is used with it, and if the hay is distributed equally among the farmers who need it most. There may even be enough for three weeks, should it turn out to be as much as or more than I expected. By that time, we surely hope, the season will be so far advanced that the weather will have changed for the better."

"So! You have already estimated the amount of hay in my stack!" said Brandur. "You have already divided this miserable little haycock among yourselves, divided it down to the very last straw. And you have weighed it almost to a gram. Then why speak to me about it? Why not take it just as it is and scatter it to the four winds? Why not?" The voice of the old man shook with anger.

"No," said Jon. "We will not do that. We want to ask your permission first. We had no intention of doing otherwise; we intended to ask you for the hay. And we did not mean to vex you, but rather to honor you in this manner. Is it not an honor to be asked to save a whole district from ruin?"

"Oh, so all this is being done to honor me!" said the old man, roaring with laughter. "Perhaps you believe me to be in my second childhood. Not at all! Old Brandur can still see beyond the tip of his nose."

The cold-heartedness shown by the old man's laughter at the distress of his fellowmen roused Jon's ire. He could see nothing laughable about the desperate situation in the district.

"Are you then going to refuse to let us have the hay,

refuse to sell it at full price, with the Parish Council guaranteeing payment?" he asked in a tone that was angry, yet under perfect control. "Is that your final answer?"

"Yes," responded Brandur. "That is my final answer. I will not let the tiny mouthful of hay I have here go while there is still life in my body, even though you mean to insure payment, and even though you actually do guarantee payment. After all, who among you will be in a position to guarantee payment if all the flocks die? The cold weather may not let up until the first of June or even later. In that case the sheep will all die. It won't go very far, this tiny haycock, not for so many. It will not, I tell you."

"But what are you going to do with the hay? If everyone else loses his flocks, everyone but you, what enjoyment will there be in owning it? And what benefit?" asked Jon.

"That does not concern me!" replied the old man. "That concerns them. It was they who decided the size of the flocks they undertook to feed this winter, not I. Besides, they could have cut as much hay as I did, even more, for they still have their eyesight. Their failure is due to their own laziness and bad judgment. That's what ails them! Ruins them!"

"But you won't be able to take this great big haystack with you into the life eternal," said Jon. "The time is coming when you will have to part with it. Then it will be used as the needs require. And what good will it do you? What are you going to do with it?"

"I am going to keep it," answered Brandur. "I intend to keep it right here on the knoll, keep it in case the haying should be poor next summer. There may be a poor growth of grass and a small hay crop; there may be a volcanic eruption and the ashes may poison the grass, as they have done in former years. Now, do you understand me?"

So saying, Brandur tottered off towards the house to indicate that the conversation was at an end. His countenance was as cold as the sky in the evening after the sun has set, and the hard lines in it resembled the streaks in the ice on rocks and ledges where the sun's rays had shone that day and laid bare the frozen ground.

Brandur entered the house, while Jon mounted again. They scarcely said a word of farewell, so angry were they both.

Jon's horse set off at a brisk pace, eager to reach home, and galloped swiftly over the hard, frozen ground. After the sun had gone down, the wind rose and a searing cold settled over the valley, whitening Jon's mustache where his breath passed over it.

Jon's anger grew as he sped along. Naturally high-tempered, he had lately had many reasons for anger since he took over his official duties. The people in his district were like people the world over: they blamed the Board constantly, accusing it of stupidity and favoritism. Yet most of them paid their taxes reluctantly and only when long overdue. Sometimes they were almost a year in arrears.

Jon reviewed the matter of the hay in his mind, also the other vexations of the past. He was sick and tired of all the trouble. And now the life of the whole district hung on a thin thread, the fate of which depended upon the whims of the weather. Jon's nose and cheekbones smarted from the cold; his shoes were frozen stiff, and pinched his feet, and his throat burned with the heat of anger rising from his breast.

Jon was rather quiet when he reached home that evening, although he did tell his wife of his attempt to deal with her father.

"Yes," said Gudrun, "papa sets great store by that hay. He cannot bear to part with it at any price. That is his nature."

"Tomorrow you must go," Jon told her, "and try to win the old man over in some way. I'd hate to be obliged to take the hay from him by force, but that will be necessary if everything else fails."

The following day Gudrun went to see her father. The weather still remained cold. When Gudrun dismounted before the house at Holl there was no one outside to greet her or announce her arrival, and so she entered, going straight into the *badstofa*. There she found her father sitting on his bed, knitting a seaman's mitten, crooning an old ditty the while:

Far from out the wilderness
Comes raging the cold wind;
And the bonds of heaven's king
It doth still tighter bind.

Gudrun leaned over her father and kissed him.

"Is that you, Gunna dear?" he asked.

"Yes, papa," she said, at the same time slipping a flask of brandy into the bosom of his shirt.

This greatly pleased the old man.

"Gunna dear," he said, "you always bring me something to cheer me up. Not many nowadays take the trouble to cheer the old man. No indeed. Any news? It's so long since you have been to see me, a year or more."

"No news everyone hasn't heard: hard times, shortage of hay, and worry everywhere. That is only to be expected. It's been a hard winter, the stock stall-fed for so long, at least sixteen weeks, on some farms twenty."

"Quite true," said Brandur. "It's been a cold winter, and the end is not yet. The cold weather may not break up before the first of June, or even Midsummer Day. The summer will be cold, the hay crop small, and the cold weather will probably set in again by the end of August, then another cold hard winter, and . . ."

He meant to go on, foretelling yet worse things to come, but Gudrun broke in: "Enough of that, father. Things can't be as bad as that. It would be altogether too much. I hope for a change for the better with the new moon next week, and mark you, the new moon rises in the south-west and on a Monday; if I remember right, you always thought a new moon coming on a Monday brought good weather."

"I did," conceded Brandur. "When I was a young man, a new moon coming on a Monday was generally the very best kind of a moon. But like everything else, that has changed with the times. Now a Monday new moon is the worst of all, no matter in what quarter of the heavens it appears, if the weather is like this—raging and carrying on so; that is true."

"But things are in a pitiful state," said Gudrun, "what with the hay shortage, almost everyone is badly off, and not a single farmer with a scrap of hay to spare, except you, papa."

"Yes, I!" answered Brandur. "I, a poor blind, decrepit old man! But what of you? Jon has enough hay, hasn't he? How is that? Doesn't he have enough?"

"Yes, we do have enough for ourselves," admitted Gudrun. "But we can't hold onto it. Jon lends it to those in need until it is all gone and there is none left for us. He thinks of others as well as of himself."

"What nonsense! What sense is there in acting like that? Every man for himself," said the old man.

"That's right. But for us that is not enough. Jon is in a position where he must think of others; he has to think of all the farmers in the district—and small thanks he gets for his pains. He is so upset, almost always on tenterhooks. He didn't sleep a wink last night—was almost beside himself. He takes it so hard."

"So Jon couldn't sleep a wink last night!" repeated Brandur. "Why be so upset? Why lie awake nights worrying about this? That doesn't help matters any. It isn't his fault that they are all on the brink of ruin."

"Quite true," answered Gudrun. "He is not to blame for that, and lying awake nights doesn't help matters, but that is Jon's disposition. He's tired to death of all the work for the Council and the everlasting fault-finding. He has had to neglect his own farm since he took up these public duties—and nothing for his time and trouble. Now this is too much. He is dead tired of it all, and so am I. In fact, I know it was worry about all this that kept Jon awake last night. We have been thinking of getting away from it all when spring comes and going to America."

"Do you side with him in this?" asked Brandur, grasping his daughter by the arm. "Do you, too, agree to his giving away the hay you need for your own flocks, giving it away until you haven't enough for yourselves? Do you, too, want to go to America, away from your father who now has one foot in the grave?"

"Yes, I do," Gudrun replied. "As a matter of fact, the plan was originally mine. If our flocks die, there will be no alternative; but if our sheep live and those of the neighbors die, our life will not be worth living because of the poverty and want round about us. Yes, papa, it was I who suggested our going. I could see no other way out."

On hearing this, Brandur's mood softened somewhat. "I expected to be allowed to pass my last days with you and your children," he said. "I cannot go on living in this fashion any longer."

"Pass your last days with us!" exclaimed Gudrun. "Have you, then, thought of leaving Holl? Have you planned to come and live with us? You've never said a word of this to me."

"I have no intention of leaving Holl. That I have never meant to do. But that is not necessary. I thought you might perhaps be willing to move over here and live with me. I could then let you have what miserable little property I have left, Gunna, my dear."

"And what about the hay, papa? Will you turn the hay over to us, the hay in the old stack? Everything depends on that."

"The hay! The hay!" the old man said. "Still harping on the hay—the hay which doesn't amount to anything and cannot be of any real help. It's sheer nonsense to think that the hay in that stack is enough to feed the flocks of a whole district. There is no use talking about it. I will not throw that tiny mouthful to all the four winds. It will do no good if divided among so many, but it is a comfort to me, to me alone. No, I will not part with it as long as there is a spark of life in me. That I will not, my love."

Brandur turned pale and the lines in his face became hard and rigid. Looking at him, Gudrun knew from experience that he was not to be shaken in his determination when in this mood. His face was like a sky over the wilderness streaked with threatening storm clouds.

Gudrun gave up. The tears rushed to her eyes, as she twined her arms around her father's neck and said: "Goodbye, papa. Forgive me if I have angered you. I shall not come here again."

The old man felt the teardrops fall on his face, the heavy woman's tears, hot with anger and sorrow.

Gudrun dashed out of the room and mounted. Brandur was left alone in the darkness at midday. Yet in his mind's eye he could see the haystack out on the knoll. He rose and went out to feel of it. It was still there. Gudrun had not ridden away with it. Brandur could hear the horseshoes crunching the hard, frozen ground as Gudrun rode off. He stood motionless for a long time, listening to the hoofbeats. Then he went into the house.

Brandur felt restless. He paced the floor awhile, stopped for a moment to raise to his lips the flask his daughter had brought him, and drained it at one gulp. All that day he walked the floor, fighting with himself until night fell.

Then he sent his foster-son with a message to his daughter. Jon, he said, had his permission to haul the hay away the very next day, but it was all to be removed in one day; there was not to be a scrap of hay or a lump of sod left by evening.

But the weather changes quickly, says an old Icelandic adage. By morning the weather had turned its spindle and the wind shifted to the south. Jon sent no messages to anyone, nor did he proclaim that the old hay was available. He first wished to see what the thaw would amount to. By the following day the whole valley was impassable because of slush and water, and the patches of earth appearing through the snowy blanket grew larger almost hourly.

Meanwhile Brandur roamed through the house all day long, asking if anyone had come. "Aren't they going to take away these miserable hay scraps? About time they came and got them!" He seemed eager that the hay be removed at once.

That day he did not take his usual walk out to the stack to feel of the hay. In fact, after that no one ever saw him show attachment to the old hay. His love of it seemed to have died the moment he granted his son-in-law permission to take it away.

That spring Brandur gave up housekeeping and of his own volition turned over the farm to his daughter and son-in-law. With them he lived to enjoy many years of good health. Never again did he take his daily walk out to the haystack to feel of the hay. But he was able to take his sip of brandy to his dying day and repeat to himself the word of God—hymns and verses from the Bible.

Now he has passed on to eternity. But his memory lives like a stone—a large, moss-covered stone by the wayside.

THE VANISHED HEROINE

TRANSLATED BY MEKKIN SVEINSON PERKINS

"SIGNY Olafsdóttir, a very old woman, native of Thingeyjar district, who lived with her daughter in the city, died here recently."

I came across this item a short time ago in a newspaper published in southern Iceland. While the noise of the spinning wheels and the children resounded in the *badstofa*, I was reading to myself.

"Any news in the paper?" asked a woman who was visiting us. She was seated at a spinning wheel. Stopping her work while she spoke, she moved the yarn to another hook on the flier.

"Nothing worth mentioning," I replied.

"Any deaths or sickness?" asked the spinner.

"Yes, here's a notice of the death of an old woman you may remember." I read the item aloud.

"I remember old Signy? Yes, indeed! So she is dead! Well, well! She was very, very old—in her nineties. May the Lord rest her soul!"

The spinning wheel started up. This visitor of ours was a hard worker.

"Where did you know her?" I asked the spinner.

She silenced the wheel suddenly. Then, gazing at me fixedly and reminiscently, she said: "Signy once stayed over night with us when we were living at Skard. It was the hard winter of 1879, or rather 1880, soon after the New Year, about the Day of the Conversion of Saint Paul. She was on her way home and intended to cross Gnupa Pass."

"Not alone?" I asked.

"Yes, alone, with the thermometer at fifteen below. And in such an outfit! No *hnjáskjól*,* and her clothes all thin and threadbare. Dressed like that, she came to our home in that piercing cold."

"Was the woman in her right mind?" I asked.

"Yes. She was very bright and always knew what she was about. But she was poor; didn't even have the clothes to cover herself. They lived in terrible misery; her husband was so shiftless."

"You say she came to your home in fifteen-below-zero weather and stayed overnight. Did she cross the pass in that biting cold, dressed like that?"

"No, not dressed like that. I did not allow her to set out in that condition. I lent her various garments in the morning. It's none of your affair what they were, neither yours nor that of any of you men. What business is it of yours?"

"You're right; that's none of my business. But did she, then, cross Gnupa Pass alone, in that bitter cold?"

"Yes. She refused company, though she carried quite a pack. It's a four-hour journey on foot and the skis clung to the snow in that terrible frost, as you can imagine. May the Lord bless her memory!"

The spinner set her wheel a-whirring and ran it at high speed until bedtime.

I went to bed that night, but not to sleep. I was quite well acquainted with Signy, and I knew Gnupa Pass thoroughly. Having ridden over it when it was well-nigh impassable, I knew every landmark in it. The pass is a vast

* Literally "knee-protector," a type of drawers formerly worn by women in Iceland.

expanse, haunted by the ghosts of the many who perished there, both long ago and in recent times.

In my thoughts I accompanied Signey over the pass during the night. Here is the account of her journey as I told it to myself.

I see her as she is leaving the house at Skard, as she is starting over Gnupa Pass, with the thermometer twenty-five below. The prevailing dead calm is of some help. But as the day advances and the sun rises higher in the heavens, how can she bear the awful glare without the protection of dark glasses?

There she goes up Kvia slope, carrying the skis in her hand and taking the slope with body stooped forward. The knapsack has already slid down on her back. The snow has been so packed by the wind that her feet sink in only slightly. Above Kvia slope Dagmala Ridge lies in the fetters of winter. Signy has the morning sun in her face as she advances. Now Skard River valley, lying athwart the mouth of the pass, opens before her. Through it runs a river, at present hidden by snow. Signy glides down from the rocky ridge to the river. She is not afraid of this place, although she has not forgotten an accident that occurred here when she was a child. A traveller broke through the ice early one mild morning, wetting his feet, and was caught in a heavy snowstorm at the mouth of the pass. There he lost his way and wandered about for three days. When at last he reached a farmhouse, both feet were so badly frozen that they had to be amputated at the instep.

Although Signy cannot shake off thoughts of this accident, she overcomes her fears. She struggles onward, and yet she looks around in all directions. On her right is a waterfall, frozen solid; the ledge is visible where the frost has made a solid cover of the falling spray. Here all is still, a dead silence reigns, broken only by the crunching of the snow underneath the skis, for they will not budge unless propelled by force. The only signs of life are seen on the snowdrifts between the peaks, where the sun's rays are reflected from the particles of snow. The effect is that of a glowing white-hot iron. But this fire is cold. It glows with the piercing cold.

Next comes the pass proper. Its mouth is very narrow, resembling a doorway. Here the path, or rather the pathless trail, cuts right across the side of a precipitous slope. Taking off her skis, Signy now grasps their points in one hand and drags them behind her, while in the other she carries her staff. Unshaken by her fears, she struggles up the precipice. In this place many a man has been lost. Here, because of the lay of the land, the winds from many directions meet. The pass cuts diagonally through the mountains. The valley lies at its mouth, and there the winds play freely, buffeting all travellers who pass through in a fog, at night, or in a snowstorm, when neither trails nor other landmarks are visible.

Above the mouth to the pass towers a lofty cliff, and on its side is a hollow. At the base of the hollow stands a huge rock, shaped like a pillar, with stones piled about it. The hollow is called Dimma Hollow and the rock Tota's Rock.

There, long ago, a poor girl was buried under the boulders, or, we might say, sent home to her own poor district in the realm of darkness. She had lost her way in a snow-storm and died of exposure. Her spirit long persisted in haunting the pass, mostly at this point, teasing travellers and hoodwinking them when it was dark. At last her ghost was laid in the hollow, or was bound to the rock. These are the two versions of the tale. The man who buried Tota under the boulders was one who was never helpless even if he had to deal with the unclean—Dean Thorleifur. It was he who drove out the evil spirit from Siglufjardar Pass.

Signy is not afraid of Tota in the universal glare from the snow, although she knows that Tota's ghost has never been completely laid. Her thoughts are full of a story told by her husband, who was never a coward.

Crossing Gnupa Pass one night when fog lay over all these boulder regions, he heard a pitiful wailing out in the fog. Skeptical of all things supernatural though he was, he at once thought of Tota and, in a loud, clear voice, called out into the night, in the direction of the cry:

"Is poor Tota awake?"

Instantly came the answer, in a voice unlike anything earthly:

"Still awake! Still alive!"

Then Signy's husband felt uneasy. He could not forget that answer or that voice. He particularly marvelled at the voice. It was so clear and trumpet-like, and yet so touchingly plaintive, as if it came partly down from the clouds and partly up from the recesses of the stony ground.

Although all these incidents are vividly present in her mind, Signy overcomes her terror. She looks up at Dimma Hollow, which is now filled with snow. Tota's Rock is clothed in a white robe, a snowdrift covering it on the side towards the trail. It has been stabbed by the sleeping-thorn of winter. The hollow, too, is wrapped in a shroud of gleaming white.

Like a worm, Tota lies there underneath the boulder. Both rock and hollow are on the right, but on the left the abyss of a jagged ravine opens directly at Signy's feet. The path is precipitous and barely wide enough for one person. There goes Signy, leaving her footprints in the packed, frozen snow, grasping the points of her skis in one hand and her staff in the other. She had tied the pack over her right shoulder in the morning, in order that it might be on the inside when she entered the pass. Unswervingly she struggles across the slope until she has passed the spot haunted by Tota's ghost.

Now Gnupa Pass opens out fully before her in all its glowing white coldness. It is a vast expanse, enclosed by boulder-strewn slopes, a whole Jotunheim in width and so long that its end cannot be seen from here.

Everything is covered with the magic blanket of white, everything except Sigga's Rock, which lies in the middle of the pass and is visible from afar. It stands on a gravel bank, which now is buried in snow. Signy directs her steps towards the rock, propelling the skis at every stroke with might and main, at the same time thrusting her staff into the snow.

Between landmarks Signy's thoughts are indefinite, that is, they have no coherence. Her mind is all set on getting onward, on getting home—home to her brood, home to the poverty. Over her breast hangs a quarter of fresh fish; on her back, the quarter of a shark, also three pounds of dark wool, a gift from the mistress of Skard, the woman now spinning in our home. The dried fish Signy got elsewhere. Once she says to herself: "If only that were home!" meaning Sigga's Rock. She sits down on the giant boulder to adjust the pack on her shoulders. She has reached the halfway point to the nearest farmhouse.

It was here that poor Sigga froze to death in a sleet storm one fall during the hard times following the eruption of 1783, barefooted, a tattered kerchief tied about her head. Signy is glad to reach the rock; she can now sit down on it for a moment of rest. The cold is piercing, and quite a stiff wind has risen. Signy wipes off the bottom of her skis with her mitten and thrusts her toes, rubbed sore by the hard, steely thongs, into the straps.

Now for the first time Signy shudders, perhaps because the wind pierced her to the skin when, exhausted, she sat down for that moment of rest, perhaps because of her thoughts. She cannot drive away thoughts of poor Sigga, who died there alone. Now Signy herself is alone. But it has not always been so. She was brought up in her father's house, where she worked hard, but in other respects led a pleasant life. There she grew into a tall, buxom, healthy young woman. Then, against her father's wishes, she married a shiftless fellow. From that day began her loneliness. She cannot complain to her father, who foretold this fate; she has no respect for her husband; her children engross her thoughts and take up her strength. On her feet she is wearing shoes someone gave her, and on her shoulders she carries gifts. Fortunately now there are people who can lend a helping hand; in Sigga's day, no one could. That was why poor Sigga lost her life by the rock in an open winter.

Signy forces her skis onward from Sigga's Rock. She does not give up. "I will! I must get there in the end," says she. "Home tonight, and bring up the children, if only it please God to spare my life!" Sigga's Rock looms high in the mighty kingdom of the snow; still higher looms the heroine on the skis.

Here Signy does not turn round to look back, though a story told by her father fills her thoughts.

He was crossing Gnupa Pass by moonlight, on the side away from Sigga's Rock. When he reached a point opposite the rock, he saw a woman, stooped and barefoot, walking on the snow. Around her head was a tattered shawl and under her arm an empty sack. Signy's father was so strong as to be a match for any two ordinary men; he could tip a cask of liquor to take a drink, and was as brave as he was strong. This vision did not frighten him in the least. In fact, he even made as if he did not see this night-prowling shade. Walking slowly to Sigga's Rock, it stopped there and seemed to disappear underneath the rock.

Signy finds it hard to fight off the cold as she gets more tired. But by this time she is well along on the second half of her journey. The condition of the snow makes skiing increasingly difficult as her strength ebbs. And the wind is more bitterly cold. Or so it seems, and so it actually is.

But now there is only one more landmark to be passed before reaching the ridge above the settlement—Einbui, a cairn which stands like a monument over a grave.

There an old man who worked for me last year fulling *vadmal* * once saw a vision. He had very queer eyes, that old man, and he had a peculiar stare when he looked around, if he thought no one saw him. Suspecting that he might be endowed with second sight, I tried to gain his confidence. I took him aside and gave him a drink. He loved that more than anything else, although he never abused it. After talking to him about this and that, I brought the conversation round to the supernatural, and then to Gnupa Pass, which is very famous for its ghosts.

"Have you ever crossed Gnupa Pass?" I asked the old man when he had been warmed with drink.

"Yes, yes, I can't deny that; I've crossed the pass, not always by daylight either."

"Did you ever see anything unusual there?" I went on.

"Yes," said he, "I saw something that was not as it should be, up there by Einbui. It was by moonlight, just before dawn. I was coming from the west; the moon was at my back and the sun about to come up. I was alone. But I have always travelled alone, then as now. The sky was cloudless and the moonlight bright. Not a shadow anywhere, for at that point in the pass the mountain slopes are low and there are no ravines. All at once I saw a man on the snow, apparently coming towards me. At first I thought it must be some traveller who had come from the east, up over the ridge, from the settlement. And yet it seemed strange how quickly he approached. In no time we had passed each other. But as he went by, I saw that he was not human. There was a transparency, a sort of mist, about him. He kept one hand in his pocket; with the

* A type of woollen cloth.

other he held his head. Then I was scared. I took to my heels and ran without stopping down to Hlidarsel, a farm right below the slope, at the foot of the pass."

Now Signy has reached Einbui and pauses to adjust the pack on her shoulders. But she does not sit down to rest. A story told by one of her lodgers runs through her mind.

He was riding past Einbui one night, his dog trotting along behind. When he approached the cairn, his horse began to snort and refused to proceed. At the same instant the dog jumped up, barking and growling as if mad. At times it would spring into the air; then again, to one side or backwards. This went on for a good while, until the traveller finally persuaded the horse to pass the spot by spurring it on a zigzag course. But the dog remained behind and was heard from afar a long time.

At last Signy reaches the eastern ridge of the pass and looks down over the settlement. "Now the Lord be praised!" says she. New life flows into her veins, though the scene before her is lifeless enough. Coming to a halt on the ridge, she allows her eyes to wander over the valley. The farmhouses are almost completely buried in snow. The only sign of life visible anywhere is the smoke, pale and thin, creeping up through the kitchen chimneys. There is less fuel than usual left in the hovels. More fires have been built lately than is customary, for inside the houses everything freezes, everything that can freeze in a farmhouse. The *skyr* * has to be cut out of the containers with an adze, carried in to the kitchen fire and thawed out, or into the

* The Icelander's favorite dessert, made of milk curds.

badstofa and kept there for a day or two, if there is the slightest bit of heat in the *badstofa*. The *slatur* * is hewn with a hand axe out of the casks—the ice broken off the top of the sausages.

Yet all containers had been covered with lids and wrapped with the greatest care. Snow had been banked up against the windows of the *badstofa* at night, and sheets of clear ice placed over the panes by day, for protection and warmth.

Even more lifeless is the scene out over the fjord. The sea is frozen solid all the way to the fishing grounds; beyond that the ice pack stretches as far as the eye can see. Countless pillars of ice are scattered about, like monuments in a graveyard. The ever-restless ocean has been stilled and solidified. It has become the graveyard of a whole world.

In silence Signy gazes upon this scene, but to her mind comes the question:

"I wonder when a boat can get into the fjord with grain for a bit of bread?"

Then with expert strokes Signy glides down the remaining slopes. But the skis refuse to glide very fast; the frost holds them back.

At last she has safely crossed the mountain pass. Unfrozen and unscathed, she has reached home with her pack, after an eight-hour journey, in a biting frost, over snow to which the skis clung.

Do you believe this tale, you, her granddaughter, who

* Blood sausages, liver sausages, heads of sheep, and other meats preserved in an acid mixture for winter use.

now live in town and have learned at school to be unlike your grandmother?

Do you think it worth the telling, you who go to the theater one night and the moving pictures the next?

Do you find it hard and tough to chew with the false teeth the dentist has put in your mouth?

Do you believe your grandmother actually made this crossing? Do you believe it, you who are too refined to walk to the sheepfold even on a summer day?

Your grandmother not only did that, but in the years that lay ahead she sat by the death bed of three grown sons and with her own hands laid them out in their coffins, yet no one saw her turn a hair. The last son fell off a cliff and was brought home, his body crushed to pieces.

Perhaps you think your grandmother rough and unfeeling.

She—the heroine? No! But she possessed great self-control. I have talked to one of the women who saw her lay out the last son, him who fell off the cliff. Your grandmother, the woman said, was like a marble statue. She could not speak. She did not shed a tear. She repressed her sobs. But her hands trembled and shook.

O Icelandic heroine! You are now resting underneath the sod. What a loss we have suffered by your death! You are a greater woman for the things you might have accomplished than for those you did accomplish, and yet your achievements would be subject enough for a large volume: all the struggle against poverty in the hovel, the rearing of your children, the sleepless nights, the work in the stables when your husband was away, and the courage not to murmur or complain.

You should be commemorated in marble in Gnupa Pass, on Sigga's Rock. There you would be avenged, both you and Sigga.

There you should stand in snow-white, ice-cold marble for ever and ever, life size, no larger. There is no need to make your statue larger than that, for you were almost six feet tall and stout in proportion. There thousands of travellers, the sons of all lands, should pass by and admire you.

And yet it would be still better if you could be born again in town and country. But that is impossible unless a new faith be adopted, a faith in a Spartan self-discipline. And that faith cannot be adopted because of our modern spirit, dazzled by the light of artificiality. You cannot be reborn because of "culture."

Gudmundur Magnússon

GUDMUNDUR MAGNÚSSON (1873–1918) was a living vindication of the truth that literary genius, coupled with the firm determination to succeed, will not in the long run be denied. He grew up in poverty, without any educational advantages, and his was for years the lot of a farm hand and fisherman. At the age of twenty he became a printer's apprentice, first in eastern Iceland and later in the capital. After spending the years 1896–1898 in Copenhagen working at a printer's trade, he returned to Reykjavík, where he made his home, plying his trade, and writing on the side the books which won for him a large reading public and still enjoy wide popularity.

Under the pen-name "Jón Trausti," he made his mark as an essayist and a lyric poet, and even tried his hand at the drama, but it is as a novelist and a writer of short stories that he has excelled. A keen observer and intimately acquainted with rural and town life, he interpreted both effectively; the former in the novel *Halla* (1906) and in the series *Heidarbýlid* (The Heath-Farm, 1908–1911); the latter notably in *Borgir* (Strongholds, 1909). His several historical novels are also noteworthy for their cultural significance. His short stories of the life of the fishermen are splendid in characterization and breathe the atmosphere of the sea; and it is in the realm of the short story that he has, on the whole, done his best work. Thus his story "Á fjörunni" (On the Beach) has been characterized as "a pearl of psychological insight and humorous narrative art."

ON THE BEACH

TRANSLATED BY MEKKIN SVEINSON PERKINS

OLD SIGMUNDUR, the watchman, hobbled out on the beach, where he was to guard the rookery.

Although his vision was dim, he could see by all signs that he had not slept too long. The danger of oversleeping is great when the tide ebbs the latter half of the night and the watchman must rise at midnight.

The tide was still at flood far up the estuary; every shallow was under water; no seaweed was visible on low rocks or reefs. Water also covered the isthmus which at low tide connected the mainland with the island where the eider ducks bred. There was now a channel, deep enough for an average ocean-going vessel.

Old Sigmundur was content. He was on time.

He forced his eyes wide open to remove the sleep from them and looked about him. Then he yawned and shook himself several times to throw off the chill that was on him and, grasping his staff with both hands, hobbled on. Old Vaskur, the watch dog, trotted along behind him, though reluctantly.

It was a bright spring night, calm and clear, yet cold and raw. Because of the chill in the air, Old Sigmundur felt he had to bundle up well. True, he possessed very few clothes, but such as they were, he had put them all on. He wore both his pairs of tattered trousers, the patched one underneath, the torn one on top; two pairs of woollen socks under his sheepskin ones and two pairs of shabby sheepskin shoes over them; a fisherman's jersey over his vest and a ragged coat on top of that. His muffler was wound several times around his neck, and on his head was a storm cap, all faded and worn. Finally, over everything he had slung his main protective garment, an oilskin coat, all tattered and torn, which was fastened with a cord around his waist.

Almost anyone would have hesitated to walk far in such an outfit, but Sigmundur was only going to the point out by the isthmus, to stand watch there till the tide came in.

To call Sigmundur "old" was not exactly accurate. He was only fifty, and did not consider himself an old man. In fact, he felt insulted when accused of being old. His spirit was still young, he said.

But he did not feel insulted when called "a poor wretch," "an unfortunate creature," "a hapless beggar," or other similar names.

He fully acknowledged his wretchedness himself. He had never amounted to much and was always sickly, though neither he nor anyone else knew exactly what ailed him. His maladies took on all manner of forms. At times an infection would develop in some part of his body; again it would be arthritis. Most frequently it was his stomach that was out of order; but sometimes it was his head, or his limbs, or his back; first one part, then another. Sigmundur was always ailing in some part.

All the quacks in two quarters of Iceland had treated him, but they had all given him up. Other doctors had never been consulted.

But what of it? Everyone could plainly see that Sigmundur was a poor wretch, no matter what ailed him, and everyone considered it his solemn duty to pity the old man and show him kindness.

Sigmundur had been born and brought up in the district. Even in youth he had been not only sickly, weak, and timid, but lazy as well. It was when he reached his twenties that his maladies began to appear. At that time, hoping to find easier work, he left home and tried many occupations, but would stick to nothing steadily. In this way he became used to roving and wandering about the country. He tramped for long throughout all of Iceland, living on the hospitality of the people and doing no work worth mentioning. Finally, when the neighboring districts began to complain about him, he was sent home and strictly forbidden to wander.

Old Sigmundur enjoyed fairly good health at this period of life. His former ailments seemed to have left him. But a new one made its appearance, and a bad one at that. Sigmundur was losing his eyesight. One eye was almost entirely blind, and the sight in the other was growing dim.

Everyone could plainly see that Sigmundur was going blind. There had been times when some insinuated that his maladies were not so serious as he claimed—though, of course, that was not true of all of them—and that his improved health was mostly due to less imaginary illness and fewer homeopathic doses.

Among those who shared this belief were the members of the local welfare board. They considered it needless to pay more than a trifle to the farmer who took the old man. They had many offers from persons who agreed to allow him to work for his board and lodging.

Yet everyone was anxious that Old Sigmundur should lead a comfortable existence and should not be abused by overwork. For that reason, when he was assigned to the farmers of Midströnd, father and son, everyone was satisfied.

Sigmundur had been at Midströnd for several years and was quite contented there.

He was an obedient creature and, in the main, got on well with everyone. Though slightly inclined to grumble, he was never ill-tempered, and usually did faithfully and obediently such work as he was able to perform. And there were quite a number of tasks he actually could do. In winter he could braid rope and weave trout and lumpfish nets. At all seasons of the year he could run errands for the womenfolk and fetch water, peat, and wood for them. He could also watch the milch ewes in summer, after they had recovered from the weaning of their lambs, and he could guard the rookery in spring.

During the breeding season of the eider ducks, when a watch was needed, Sigmundur was expected to devote himself entirely to that. He could sleep during high tide, or do whatever else he wished with that time, provided he was on watch during low tide. He had, as a matter of fact, to be on duty only during the night ebb tide; in the daytime there were always people about and the fox was not likely to attack the rookery then.

So Sigmundur's work was not very hard. It merely required his staying on the point and making a noise to frighten away the fox. There was no danger of its getting over to the island elsewhere.

Vaskur, an old house dog, had been assigned to Sigmundur to help with this work. The old man was to yell and sick on the dog, and the dog was to bark loudly. Nothing more was needed, for the fox was so foolish as to believe that some danger must lurk there and dared not come near.

But Sigmundur and Vaskur did not get on well together. Quite often Vaskur would deceive the old man and quietly sneak off home, which, of course, made matters worse, for then Sigmundur had to do the work of both, sicking and barking alternately. This he did so realistically that even the fox was deceived.

During flood tide Sigmundur usually went home to eat and rest. Yet not infrequently, instead of going home, he would stroll over to a neighboring farm, Insta-Strönd. Eirikur, the farmer there, always received him kindly and bade him welcome. But as it was almost equally far to Insta-Strönd and Midströnd, Sigmundur was at times too lazy to go to either house, and would sleep through the flood tide in his shack on the point. No one worried if he failed to come home at that time.

Though a poor specimen of manhood, weak physically, wretched and poverty-stricken, Sigmundur possessed one talent envied by many richer and greater men, a talent money cannot buy. He was a rhymester.

To have called him a poet would have been an exaggeration. No one did that, not even in jest. He made no claim to such a title himself, at least not yet. But whether he had given up hope that perhaps some day he might—that was another matter.

No one denied that Sigmundur was a rhymester, and quite a good one, too, when compared with other rhymesters in the district. From childhood he had shown a very strong bent towards poetry and had possessed a deep yearning to produce something in that line. But his circumstances were straitened. He received no education whatever in his youth and he found it difficult to obtain one later. Consequently his progress in the poetic art was slow.

Yet some of his verses had been spread by word of mouth, memorized, and recited in various quarters—particularly some harmless satirical verses about this one or that one. And a whole "whale ballad" had become public, though it was rather hushed up. It told a *hvalfjörusaga* * which could be repeated only in secret because of the persons concerned. For that very reason a great many were eager to hear it.

It was only during the last few years that Sigmundur had attained such perfection in his art. Year by year he felt a steady improvement and began to hope that he would at last reach his long-desired aim—that somebody whose word counted in such matters would call him a poet some time before he died.

Although rather imperfect, this art of his brought Sigmundur many a happy hour and helped to lighten his wretchedness. It may have played an important part in bringing about the improvement in health which he enjoyed during the last few years and it was the reason for his wishing to stave off old age as long as possible.

Besides composing original poetry, Old Sigmundur knew by heart no end of verses and related anecdotes, whole lays and ballads which this one or that one had composed and which were hard to get, and he was always

* Literally a "whale-beach story." Whenever a whale is beached, word is sent throughout the countryside summoning the inhabitants to assist in cutting up the carcass and to share in the spoils. Dramatic incidents occurring on such occasions are the subject of a "whale-beach story."

willing to recite them for all who were willing to listen.

Then, too, he had wandered far and wide, and could tell many unusual tales. He had seen many men, and had even met noted personalities in distant parts of the country, such as Bólu-Hjálmar,* the poetaster Niels, and many others. Although no one doubted that his poetic imagination somewhat colored his stories about these men, it was entertaining to listen to him now and again, and especially to see the old man, who would become so exalted with joy, enthusiasm, and poetic inspiration that his blind eye glowed like the eye of a haddock in the dark.

At home at Midströnd there was no great enthusiasm for the tales and verses of Old Sigmundur; his masters had long since heard enough of them.

At Insta-Strönd, on the contrary, he got a much better hearing. Old Eirikur was an intelligent man and a connoisseur of all such things. He knew all manner of interesting folk tales and anecdotes himself, and was always eager to hear anything new of the sort.

Their common zeal for poetry and tales drew the two old men together, although their circumstances were quite different in other respects, Eirikur being a prosperous farmer. It was because of this common interest that Old Sigmundur was always welcome at Insta-Strönd; it was also because of it that he often strolled over there.

Naturally Eirikur was bored if he had to hear too many of the verses of Sigmundur at one time. But as the old watchman was such a poor wretch and as he almost always told something that was entertaining, Eirikur felt in duty bound to receive him kindly and encourage him.

* A noted peasant poet.

Sigmundur considered Eirikur the only friend he had in the whole world and loved him devotedly. All his verses were written with but one aim in mind: to please Eirikur. And when he had composed something fine, or when some good story had occurred to him, he would as a matter of course at once rush over to Insta-Strönd to submit it to Eirikur.

When he chanced to find Eirikur in a good mood, or when he told something especially pleasing to the master of Insta-Strönd, the latter would call him into the best room —after ordinary refreshments had been served—and give him a sip from his flask. Then Old Sigmundur was so delighted that he could not restrain himself. He would rush up to Eirikur and kiss him.

When he left the house at Insta-Strönd after a reception of this kind, carrying a load of food which the housewife had given him to take along to the beach—a bundle so large that his oilskin coat bulged in front above the cord as though it covered a large pack—Old Sigmundur was in high spirits. Then he was indeed content with his lot and experienced the joy that comes from being poetical and well versed in lore.

Many would stare at Old Sigmundur when he walked to the beach in the costume we have already described. He always walked with a plain stick or mattock handle, which he grasped in both hands and pricked into the ground in front of him at every step, never actually taking the step until the stick had a firm hold. His gait thus became a constant series of forward pulls and jerks. At a distance the old man's mood could easily be discerned from the manner in which he walked. When he was in good spirits, or when the muse was working, he would walk like a berserk, the pulls and jerks almost disappearing. But when he was downcast, he would drag himself forward by his stick, like a feeble old man in his nineties, coming to a complete halt between jerks.

On the occasion we have just described, Sigmundur was in a cheerful mood, and he walked briskly in the direction of the point.

Vaskur, on the other hand, was in a bad humor. Yet he did set out with the old man. He trotted along slowly behind him a little more than half way to the point, falling farther and farther behind. In the end, he silently turned round and sauntered home.

But Sigmundur reached his destination, the end of the point, in good time.

The shack intended for the watchman on the point would have deserved being placed on exhibition at a world's fair. A more remarkable building could not be found though a search were made from pole to pole. It was hardly right to call it a shack; the name was too dignified. It was a double-walled shelter built of rubble. In its construction, stones, both large and small, had been perched loosely on one another with little or no skill; in some places seaweed had been stuffed between the stones to hold them together, and the space between the inner and outer wall had been filled with gravel. Here and there, backbones of whale, old and weathered, had been used, each one taking the place of several stones and imparting a grotesque appearance to the whole structure. These magnificent, workmanlike walls formed a distorted quadrangle, with a door facing the south.

Rafters or driftwood and whale ribs, crisscrossed irregularly and perched loosely one on the other, making the roof bulge inward in some places, but outward in others, had been placed on top of these remarkable walls. Over the pile of loosely laid rafters and whale ribs, flat stone slabs from the hill near the beach had been placed, then a layer of seaweed, and lastly stones and whale bones on top of the seaweed, to hold it down. The roof formed a crest-shaped thatch, which at first would shed the rain, but afterwards when the seaweed had become saturated, so held the water that it would leak for a long time after the rain had stopped.

The watchmen who had preceded Old Sigmundur had built this shack; it was therefore not the work of any one man. Sigmundur himself had added to it and patched it since he took over the watch, but its appearance had not improved in his day.

Beside this grotesque hovel Sigmundur came to a halt and looked about him.

The weather was heavenly—a dead calm and the water smooth as far as the eye could see. Only a few tiny waves played upon the beach, for Aegir * never sleeps so soundly as not to show some signs of life in most places along the shores of Iceland. These wavelets kept ploughing up the heap of seaweed that extended all along the shore and formed a shelf or ledge along the highwater mark. Only at high tide could the water reach it; at low tide a wide expanse of sandy beach stretched out beyond it. Now the waves passed, unbroken, up to this seaweed barrier, sending a brown pulpy mash flying into the air. The whole scene

* The god of the sea.

before him reminded Sigmundur that he had waked up in good time and that the tide had ebbed only a little.

The sky was somewhat overcast. A thin veil of clouds covered the ocean; only a trace of sun was visible behind the clouds. On the other side of the bay the mountains stood out blue and clear. All the crevasses on the mountain-sides were still filled with snow, but the peaks and crags were a deep purple, and the stillness of night lay over everything.

The channel was quite broad when the tide was so high over the isthmus, and the chances were slight that the fox would attempt such a long swim. At a distance the island appeared to be covered with a dense forest, which in reality was composed of the scarecrows—poles with tufted branches at the top, set up to frighten away birds of prey from the rookery and to shelter the eider ducks during the breeding season. Above the water's edge the whole island was covered with scurvy-cress and succulent forage grasses. This gave it the appearance of having spread over it a carpet of yellowish-green velvet in which the eider ducks slept. The females were not visible from the main-land; the males looked like white cotton-grass balls dotting the whole island.

The island itself stood clearly reflected in the channel.

Peace and quiet reigned, as if all the inhabitants had decided to sleep later than usual. Here and there, a tern could be seen fluttering over the forest of scarecrows, probably out hunting a morsel for breakfast, somewhere beyond the highwater mark. But it had sense enough to keep quiet. Silent and philosophical, a few eider drakes were swimming in the dark green shadow cast by the island.

They had to be very still, for "mama" was sitting on the eggs in the nest and the least they could do was to see to it that she had peace at night.

Sigmundur was so enchanted by the stillness and beauty of the night that he could not persuade himself to sick on the dog and bark; that, he felt, would be profaning such a lovely spring night, an unseemly disturbance of a mighty peace.

He contemplated the scene again and again without growing weary of it. Somehow his shack seemed incongruous to him at the moment.

But within him he felt an indefinable commotion that nothing before him could satisfy. He was tormented by a vague yearning which he was unable to shake off. It came over him in great waves, like a storm, again and again, each wave more powerful than the last.

In the end Old Sigmundur discovered what ailed him. It was the poetic urge. The muse had descended upon him. The beauty of the night had awakened the poetry in his soul.

At first he paced the beach for a time, slipping on the pebbles and stumbling at every step. But such a gait was not the best for one in his state of mind. Stumbling so often tended to disturb his thoughts. When his walk was jerky, his thoughts too were inclined to be jerky. In the end he decided to go inside the shack and sit down on a soft heap of seaweed that lay in one of the corners.

He knew, of course, that the watchman was not supposed to stay inside, except occasionally in the very worst weather. But having often broken that regulation without suffering any serious consequences, he considered it a matter of course that he should now go inside, for a short time at least.

Having settled himself comfortably on the heap of seaweed, he stuffed some of it behind his back, to form a soft cushion there, and, stretching out his legs, he placed them on the soft seaweed too. When he had shaken himself, rested for a while, and was as comfortable as the circumstances permitted, the muse began to work.

He soon found the subject for his poem: his shack and its surroundings, himself, and the watch over the rookery.

Never before had it occurred to him to compose a poem about that, and yet it was an excellent subject. He doubted not that he could make an unusually fine poem about it. And if he should make a really fine one, he firmly resolved to stroll over to Insta-Strönd during the next flood tide. Eirikur had recently made a trip to the village.

The blood rushed through his veins at the thought and a favorable wind lifted both wings of the muse.

He began with a description of his surroundings.

The central point was his shack, built of rubble and the backbone of whale, with rafters of spruce and willow, ridge pole of whale rib and thatch of stone slabs, seaweed, and gravel, like the funeral pyre of some ancient hero. Grotesque and poetic it was, and yet "a lookout palace," "a defensive castle," "the boat-house of his Fjalar's fley." He could characterize it by all these kennings.* In the poetic

* *Kennings* are the poetic circumlocutions which were used in great numbers in skaldic verse. Some of them are far-fetched and so complex as to be difficult to understand, but many are full of subtle and profound thought. Snorri Sturluson, in his instructions to young poets, lists a great many, such as for instance: heaven, Skull of Ymir; the earth, Odin's Bride; the sea, Encircler of

language it was "the whalebone roof-hole boar," "the narwhale-rib boat-house," "the stone castle thatched with the hair of the skerry-field," "the castle where the waves of Bodn * around the benches flowed," "the fortress raised by giant hands," and so forth.

What would Eirikur of Insta-Strönd say to that?

And this remarkable poetic castle of whalebone, seaweed, and stone slabs was not lonely and deserted in the poem. Sigmundur was there himself, the defending hero, the main character of the whole lay.

He was the defender of the land, like Ulfar the Strong or Högni in the Andra Lay, clad in mail and fully armed, strong of limb and skilled in war. Fearless, almost a werewolf and troll-eyed was he, if need be, and so terrifying that the birds of prey and the wild beasts of the land fell back before him.

There were a great many kennings for himself which mature poetic art, based on the Edda, placed at his disposal. He was "the bearer of the shield," "the oak of the target," "the swayer of the wound-ripper," "the ash of Omi's armor," "the wielder of the sword," "the bender of the bow," "the king of Bodn's mead," "the king of the whale-bone castle." These and many other yet more poetic kennings could be applied to him, if need be. Fortunately he had been christened Sigmundur, an Odin's name, which in itself could serve as a kenning. This gave him "Sigmundur of the sun on the estuary," "Sigmundur of

Islands; the sun, Sister of the Moon; the wind, Wolf of the Wind; summer, Comfort of Serpents; gold, Hair of Sif, Freyja's Tears, and so on.

* The poetic mead.

the pit's gleam," * "Sigmundur of the blood of Son," † or at least always the Sigmundur who fought and threatened, composing poetry the while. His oilskin coat became a ring-byrnie; his tattered trousers turned into greaves; his staff was a *dragvendill* ‡ or a mace alternately, as required by the subject and the rhyme, and many of the kennings from the Edda could be applied to it. Old Vaskur, the dog, could not be left out, though he had, to be sure, deceived Sigmundur and run home. He was magnified and became a tame forest bear. He had to be comparable in size to everything else; an ordinary dog was far too small to accompany such a hero.

And when "Son-liquor Sigmundur" or "wound-stick Sigmundur" stood on guard, clad in byrnie and greaves, with the mace on his shoulder and a savage bear at his side, it was, of course, to be inferred that the rookery would be properly guarded.

Never before had Sigmundur done anything comparable to this!

The kingdom he had to defend was the rookery. There King Eider reigned, with the ducks as the ladies of his court. In that kingdom there was more beauty and splendor, more wealth and gentleness than heroism. Though the king himself was a peaceful man, not inclined to bold undertakings, his kingdom was constantly in danger of attacks by vikings and robbers, trolls and monsters, which so harried the land and ravaged the coast that a powerful force was required to hold them back.

* A kenning meaning "rich man."

† A kenning meaning "the poet."

‡ A famous sword.

The tern, who likewise dwelt on the island, was a troublesome servant, not especially pleasing to the poet—always ill-tempered, always grumbling, and always trying to meddle in the defense. She could not appreciate this great hero, nay, was even sure to cast dirt on him, if she had the chance.

The foes that Sigmundur had to combat were far from insignificant. There were vultures so large that they could easily seize an average man in their claws and devour him whole, crushing his arms and armor in their beaks and pulverizing his bones. The foxes became warlike wolves, running in dense packs over the hill and disturbing the peace. At the head of each pack was a huge leader, as large as a tiger and much more terrifying, with a human face, claws of steel, and teeth unlike anything earthly.

Sigmundur had to ward off these monsters which fell upon him as he stood on guard. It was quite evident what a terrific battle would ensue!

Wonder what Eirikur of Insta-Strönd would say to that? thought Sigmundur.

Never had his imagination taken such a flight. He was not "Old" Sigmundur now; nothing could be more ridiculous than to call him that. Now he was "Young" Sigmundur. Such flights of fancy are not natural to the old.

The meter he had chosen was the most difficult one he knew, but that mattered not to him. He progressed rapidly, overcoming every obstacle that came in his way. The rhymes fell together and fitted into each other almost of themselves. The poetic kennings attacked Sigmundur as thick and fast as swarms of mosquitoes. He had scarcely time to select from them the best. Yet in such selection lay the poetic art. A wealth of words welled up within him, a wealth so great that he could hardly believe it himself. And if the ordinary everyday words were hard to manipulate and refused to fall easily into place, it was an old poetic device to trim them down, cutting off their worst corners, patching them up, or stretching them a bit, until they would fit. This was indeed a permissible poetic license.

Thus the poem grew rapidly, minute by minute.

If only he would find Eirikur of Insta-Strönd in good spirits, preferably a little "happy" with drink! When in that condition, Eirikur was always in the very best humor. And if Eirikur was happy, and if he liked the poem, there was no doubt as to what he would do. He would, of course, call Sigmundur into the best room and open the large green trunk. And there was no uncertainty as to what would happen next. The throat of Old Sigmundur would not be totally parched when he went out on the watch the next flood tide!

But to return to the poem.

Sigmundur was not certain that Eirikur would consider the lines already completed quite forceful enough. They had to be made more forceful, so that the old man could really appreciate them.

Sigmundur, therefore, began racking his brain for something to impart more life to his poem. The right thing occurred to him almost at once: the ocean, the sea—not as it was at the moment, fast asleep; it was impossible to write poetry about it in that state—but rather as it was when raging in all its might and fury.

All the kennings for the sea rushed into the mind of Sigmundur. It was "the jotun's blood," "the blood of

Mimir's veins," "the swollen encircler of the islands," "the son of Loki," and "Aegir's wife in giant form." There Aegir, Ran, and their daughters held drinking parties and frolicked turn about. The Midgard Serpent thrashed about in the deep, blowing fire and venom from its nostrils and violently churning up the waves, which, white-maned and hideous, rushed screaming up to the rock where waged the combat between the berserk defending the land and the attacking monsters. Meanwhile, Hraesvelgur * stood at the world's end, flapping his wings and urging all the monsters of the deep on to the attack. Then "cat whales," cachalots, "horse whales," narwhals, blue whales, "ling backs," combers, and "red combs," † came rushing out of the sea. And basking shark and crested seal were not wanting. Mermen with large lidless eyes waded up to their nipples in water twenty fathom deep, and sea monsters, large as churches, covered with shell and with glass windows in their bodies, rushed up on the beach and with wide open mouths stood gaping at the combat.

Before the poet rose in mental picture the face of Eirikur of Insta-Strönd listening to this description.

Everything fitted beautifully into the poem. Never had Sigmundur composed anything so masterly! Never had his art risen to such heights!

He stopped now and then to review what he had completed and to repeat it to himself. How happy it all made him!

Then he went on, entirely forgetting himself in his exultation, enraptured by his success and by the riches of his

* From the Edda, a carrion swallower.

† Various monsters of whose very existence there is doubt.

mind. It was as though the goddess of poetry herself had appeared before him in all her grace and glory, to open up her world to him, and was enticing him ever farther and farther into the realm of immortal art.

"Look at the old fool! He's asleep!"

Sigmundur woke with a start and looked up—his masters! The face of Grimur appeared in the doorway and beside it the head of Thorvaldur came immediately into view with the shaggy gray hair sticking out from beneath his cap and the gray whiskers encircling his jaws like a collar.

"Get out of here, you deceitful dog!" screamed old Thorvaldur, in a furious rage. "You ought to be beaten till every bone in your body was smashed to bits!"

Sigmundur stumbled down off the heap of seaweed and rose to his feet with remarkable speed, despite the stiffness in his joints. Then he went outside to face his masters. When he got there, he was overwhelmed with curses and questions, though not actually beaten.

Old Sigmundur felt so surprised at all this that he was at his wit's end. He realized, of course, that the pesky old fox must have played him a trick while he was busy composing his poetry. He also realized that it would be useless to tell his masters what he had been doing. That would only make matters worse. So he decided to invent excuses, or at least to beg for mercy. But the tongue clove to the roof of his mouth; though he tried again and again everything that occurred to him, he always had to stop before he was half through. So flustered was he as to be entirely beside himself. After stammering for a while, in the end he burst into tears.

What had actually happened from the moment when Sigmundur's consciousness said farewell to this deceitful world till he was awakened by that rude greeting was briefly this.

The fox, which was neither a wolf nor a monster, but only a ravenous, lean vixen, had crept out of her lair on the hill and gone in search of food. As usual, she had her sharp ears along. Though she pricked them up well, she heard nothing to give her cause for fear. She had turned in the direction of the sea, for there, she knew, was her best chance of finding something. Then she wandered along the shore to a point near the island. She had been there often before at that time of night, but had always become aware of something that made approach seem inadvisable.

Coming to a halt on the hillside, she looked toward the bright green island, alive with ducks and densely covered with nests. What a tempting sight it was!

Though she strained her eyes and pricked up her ears, she could neither see nor hear anything to arouse her fears or her suspicion. Then it was that temptation overcame her. Running lightly down the slope on to the point behind the watchman's shack, she stepped cautiously out on the beach, taking care not to make a sound. Then she dived into the channel.

Despite her sharp eyes and good ears, the vixen had overlooked a tiny flat-bottomed boat which lay in the shadow of the land, a short distance from Midströnd. In it were Thorvaldur and his son Grimur, out examining their lumpfish nets. They had risen unusually early, for Grimur intended to go fox-hunting up on the moor after having tended to the nets. For that reason he had a loaded gun in the boat with him.

When old "short-legs" landed on the island, an indescribable, hellish racket arose out there. The drakes escaped first, rushing in all directions and leaving a large area around the beast bare. Then, one by one, the ducks flew off their nests, quacking and screaming in deadly terror, even before the fox approached them. One of the ducks was in such headlong haste that she failed to look where she was going, and flying full force against a scarecrow, was instantly killed.

The terns, too, were frightened off their nests, but they had no intention of fleeing. They were bold enough to attack the uninvited guest and do what damage they could. Although one lone tern can accomplish but little, it is quite a different story when many of them work together. The pesky vixen got into the direst straits under the attack of that flock of terns. Even before she had time to suck two or three eggs, her whole body was bleeding from wounds inflicted by sharp tern bills.

The farmers of Midströnd immediately noticed the disturbance on the island. They also immediately saw that a fox, and not a bird of prey, was causing it. They could even see where the fox was, for the terns formed a pillar straight above her head. Flying high into the air, these small gray shrews would swoop screeching down upon the fox and, with wide open bills, attack her in full force. Then they would fly back again to renew the attack.

The farmers rowed over to the island at once and came to the assistance of the terns.

When the vixen became aware of the presence of men on the island, she saw at once that the game was up and took to her heels. Eager to save the dead duck, she seized it in her mouth, but soon realized the impossibility of making her escape with it, and dropped it. Then she dived into the channel.

She was only a few fathoms from land when the shot rang out. Although the balls cut the surface of the water right by her nose, not one of them hit her.

With a great spurt she rushed ahead, though there was no need for such haste. An old worn muzzle-loader is not quickly reloaded.

But, on the other hand, it was not encouraging to see the boat in pursuit. The vixen was fast losing her strength and would not long be able to make great spurts.

On came the boat, ever nearer and nearer, ploughing a furrow of foam through the glassy surface of the water. While Thorvaldur alone pulled at the oars, it moved quite swiftly, and it fairly leaped forward once Grimur had taken an oar.

Although the farmers quickly reduced the distance between themselves and their quarry, it was not till they reached land that they caught up with her. A tremor of fright ran through the frame of the little brown creature when she saw Grimur brandishing an oar. She could no longer put on enough speed to escape; her strength was almost exhausted. Striking her on the tail, which dragged behind in the water, the oar handle injured her badly. But at the next stroke, it hit a stone in the bottom and broke with a loud crash.

Before Grimur could seize the other oar, the vixen had crept up on the beach. Although by that time her strength was about spent, Grimur and his father were unable to catch her once she had firm ground under her feet.

Pursuers and pursued were thus separated, and the fox made her escape. But she was so terrified that she doubtless long remembered the experience and never again was deceived by a treacherous night calm.

Having lost the fox, Grimur and his father began searching for Sigmundur, the watchman, and took out their spite on him.

"Get you gone! Home with you, you confounded cheat! You'll never be entrusted with this work again!"

Shamefaced, Sigmundur hobbled off in the direction of home.

The first part of the way he was quite dejected. He dragged himself along, leaning forward on his stick, half whimpering and thinking only of his wretchedness. He felt sick all over, more miserable than any beast on earth.

But as he proceeded, he began to feel calmer. He knew that, though his masters were angry with him at the moment, which was only natural because of the unfortunate accident, they would not remain so for long. He also knew that if he went to them and asked their forgiveness for this blunder, they were not the men to drive out a poor sickly old man and refuse to give him work. And even if they did, Sigmundur doubted not that his friend, Eirikur of Insta-Strönd, would help him in some way, were his aid sought.

By the time Sigmundur was half way home, his gait had become much smoother, in fact almost normal.

But worst of all, he had forgotten every word of his magnificent lay. The unfortunate accident had so upset him that he could not recall one word of that masterpiece. The connection between it and his memory had been completely severed.

"WHEN I WAS ON THE FRIGATE"

TRANSLATED BY MEKKIN SVEINSON PERKINS

I WAS stormbound in the village. I had arrived there with the steamer, and now the steamer had gone, but I was left behind, a stranger, at a loss what to do.

It was my intention to continue my travels across country, mostly through the mountainous region on the other side of the fjord. Neither horse nor guide for the journey had yet been found. Storms and floods made all preparations difficult. It was spring, at Crouchmas time.

I was staying at the home of the doctor. He had taken me in and was trying to help me in various ways. Now he was in my room. We sat there chatting and smoking our cigars. Having given up all hope of continuing my journey that day, I had made myself comfortable on the doctor's couch.

When least expected, someone in seamen's boots came tramping into the vestibule, and there was a knock on the door.

"Come in," called the doctor. The door opened gently, and a young man, clad in oilskins, stood in the doorway.

"I was asked to tell you that the stranger can get passage over the fjord with Old Hrolfur of Stifla, if he wishes," said the man, addressing the doctor.

We both stood up, the doctor and I, and went to the door. This solution of my problem had not occurred to either of us.

"Is Old Hrolfur going to the fishing grounds now?" asked the doctor.

"Yes, he is going to the islands and will be there for about a week. 'Twould be no trouble at all for him to put the stranger ashore in the Mula Valley, if that would be of any help."

"Fine!" said the doctor. Then turning to me: "You should consider this offer, if you do not absolutely have to go round the head of the fjord. It will save you at least a whole day's journey, and you'll find it easier to get a horse and guide in the Mula Valley than here."

All this had so taken me by surprise that I was not prepared to answer at once. I looked from the doctor to the visitor, and my first thought was that the doctor wished to get rid of me. Then I began thinking how fine it would be if I could in this way avoid crossing all the rivers that empty into the head of the fjord. In the end, I decided that the doctor's advice was actuated solely by kindness.

"Is Old Hrolfur quite right just now?" the doctor asked, turning to the man in the doorway.

"Oh, yes, indeed," was the reply.

"Quite right?" I asked, looking with inquiring eyes at them. To me the question seemed peculiar.

The doctor smiled.

"He is slightly out of order here," he explained, pointing at his head.

The idea of setting out on a long trip by sea with a crazy man made me shudder. I am sure the doctor read my thoughts, for he smiled good-naturedly.

"Is it safe to go with him?" I asked.

"Yes, quite. He is not insane. Far from it. He is merely a little queer; has bats in the belfry, as the saying goes. At times he is mentally affected when forced to stay at home in the dead of winter with nothing to occupy his mind; but in summer there are few signs of it. And he is an excellent sailor."

"Yes, an absolutely dependable steersman," said the man in the doorway. "It is perfectly safe to go to sea with him now. I'll guarantee that."

"Are you going with him?" asked the doctor.

"Yes, there are three of us with him, four altogether in the boat."

I looked more closely at the fellow in the doorway. He was a promising young man, about twenty and well poised. His appearance impressed me very favorably.

In fact, I began to feel ashamed of not daring to cross the fjord with three men like him, even if the skipper was queer in the head.

"Are you going today?" asked the doctor. "Don't you think it's too stormy?"

"Old Hrolfur won't let that hold him back," said the man, smiling.

"Is it fit for sailing?"

"I should say so, and a fine fair wind."

In the end it was decided that I should go with them, and I hurriedly began making preparations. My baggage and riding equipment were carried down to the boat.

When I left, the doctor walked to the landing with me.

There, in the shelter of the jetty lay Old Hrolfur's boat, its mast raised and the sail wrapped round it. A four-oared boat of the larger type it was, tarred all over except the gunwale, which was painted a light blue. In the boat itself were various pieces of tackle used in shark fishing, among others a large bultow pole with four hooks of wrought iron, a cask of shark bait from which the vilest odor rose, and barrels to receive the shark liver. Shark knives lay under the thwarts and large gaff hooks were hooked beneath the ribs. The boxes containing the provisions of the crew were placed in the prow.

In the stern the back of a man was visible. He was bending over, arranging stones in the bottom of the boat. He was clad in a pair of leather breeches which extended up under his armpits, with cords that were crossed and passed over his shoulders. In the prow stood another man, and a third was on the wharf.

"Good morning, my dear Hrolfur," said the doctor.

"Good morning," replied Hrolfur curtly, as he straightened up and spat a streak of tobacco juice. "Hand me that stone there."

The last few words were addressed to the man on the wharf, neither to the doctor nor myself. Hrolfur cast a brief, unfriendly glance at me, but otherwise he seemed to take no notice of me. I felt as if I had been stabbed when those piercing, harsh eyes looked at me. No one has ever given me a more piercing or harsher look.

Hrolfur was a short, thickset man, now beginning to age. His face was thin and quite wrinkled, his skin tanned and weatherbeaten, and a straggly unkempt beard grew around his mouth. I at once noticed a strange twitching of his face, apparently the after-effects of alcoholic fits. He wore a hard, melancholy expression. His hands were swollen and toil-worn, calloused by many years of rowing.

"Don't you think it's stormy, my dear Hrolfur?" asked the doctor after a long silence.

"Oh, not so bad," replied Hrolfur, without looking up.

Here the conversation was broken off again. Hrolfur did not seem inclined to talk, not even with the district physician.

The doctor looked at me and grinned. He conveyed the impression that Old Hrolfur was exactly as he had expected to find him.

"I hope you'll be kind enough to help this traveller, my dear Hrolfur," said he, after quite a long silence.

"Oh, well, carrying him will make little difference in the boat."

In other words, I should merely be additional ballast.

"Don't you think it will be hard to land in the Mula Inlet?"

Hrolfur straightened up and rested his hand on his back.

"Hang it, no, not at all," he said. "There's an off-shore wind, the water's smooth, and we'll probably get there at flood tide."

"Won't it take you out of your way?" I asked.

"Not much. We'll get there for all of that. Rowing on the inlet is mere play to us."

Presently I said farewell to the doctor and slid down

into the boat. The fisherman who was still standing on the wharf untied the mooring rope and, throwing it into the boat, jumped in after it. One of the sailors thrust the handle of an oar against the wharf to shove the boat off. Then they rowed into the wind for a short distance, while Old Hrolfur hooked the rudder on.

The sail bellied out and, leaning smoothly to one side, the boat ran in a wide curve. The small islands at the mouth of the harbor raced past us.

We steered for the open bay. On the horizon the headlands rose straight out of the sea, a deep purple, with thick, dishevelled caps of fog on their heads. It was a long, hard pull out there.

Hrolfur was at the helm. He sat in the stern, on a crossbeam flush with the gunwale, resting each foot on one of the ribs and holding the tiller lines outside his legs, one on either side.

I was in the prow, by the mast, with the fishermen. We all knew from long experience that Icelandic boats sail better when well loaded forward. We lay, all four of us, to windward, and yet the spume seethed over the oarlocks on the leeward.

"If you think we're not going fast enough, boys, you'll have to put out the oars, gratis," said Hrolfur, grinning.

We took this joke well. In fact, it seemed to draw me closer to the old man. Before that I had been somewhat afraid of him. Jokes always have the effect of an extended hand.

For a long time little was said. We crouched silently before the mast, Old Hrolfur in the stern; the whole length of the boat lay between us.

The fishermen did their utmost to make me comfortable. I lay on soft bags right in front of the thwart, my head protected by the gunwale. The spray splashed over my head and fell into the bottom of the boat on the leeward.

The young man who had come for me at the doctor's home had nestled down in the prow forward of me. His name was Eirikur Eiriksson. I liked him better all the time.

Another fisherman sat on the thwart, his back resting against the mast. He, too, was a young man, just growing his first down. Ruddy of face, quiet of manner and indolent, he budged not in the least though one shower of spray after another flew right in his face.

The third member of the crew lay down crosswise in the boat behind the thwart, pillowed his head on his folded oilskin, and dropped off to sleep.

For a long time, almost an hour, I lay there in silence, thinking only of what I heard and saw about me. And that was more than enough to keep me awake.

I saw how the mainsail arched out, full of wind, and pulled hard at the clew-line, which was attached to the gunwale beside Hrolfur. The jib was like a beautifully curved iron plate, stiff and unyielding. Both sails were snow white, semi-transparent, and gentle in every movement, like the ivory sails of the ship models in Rosenborg Palace. As the mast bent over, the stays on the windward were taut like the strings of a harp. The boat shivered like a leaf. Through the thin clincher work I felt the pounding against my cheek, though I didn't get wet. Between sharp blows, the waves would pat us very gently. Once in a while I could see foaming white crests above the gunwale on the leeward. At times I saw the horizon underneath the sails, but more frequently I saw only the back of a broad wave which the boat had ridden and from which it had only just jumped down.

The boat rolled very slightly. Held steadily at an even angle, it ploughed through the waves. There was merely an agreeable motion, soothing to the nerves, quite unlike the wide pitching of large ships.

Our conversation gradually started up again. Eirikur proved to be the most talkative, and the man on the thwart put in a word now and then.

The talk turned to Old Hrolfur.

We lowered our voices so that he should not hear us, although, as a matter of fact, there was no need to fear that; we were so far away from him and the wind was bound to carry our words to one side. But people always lower their voices when speaking about those within sight, even when speaking only well of them.

I hardly took my eyes from Hrolfur. What the fishermen told me about him gradually explained him to me.

He sat there in silence, holding the lines and staring straight before him. At least he took no notice of us.

Briefly, what the fishermen told me was this:

Hrolfur had been reared in the village and had lived nowhere else. His cottage stood by the dam in the river and had been named Stifla after it.

Whenever possible, he followed the sea, catching shark in the spring, cod and haddock in other seasons of the year. He was content nowhere except at sea. If he could not go to sea, he would stay alone at home in his cottage, mending his fishing tackle. He never worked by the day, as so many fishermen did, and he never hired out at haying time. Humming and talking to himself, he would putter about his fish-shed, his boathouse, and his hut, his hands covered with tar and fish grease. When spoken to, he gave curt, often peevish, at times even abusive replies. Hardly anyone dared go near him.

And yet everyone liked him. Everyone who knew him said he improved surprisingly on acquaintance. His eccentricity had become worse with age, they said, especially since he lost his son.

His son had been a very promising young fellow and was considered the bravest of all the fishermen in the village. He always rowed out farthest and, of course, brought back the largest catch. One day a heavy gale sprang up while he was far out to sea, away beyond the mouth of the fjord. Though it took a hard pull against tide and wind to reach land, he and his crew managed to row up to the headland, but by that time they were all exhausted. They decided to attempt a landing in the Mula Inlet. Unfortunately, the boat capsized at the mouth of the inlet. Hrolfur's son was drowned, as was one of the other men, but the rest were rescued.

For a long time after this accident Hrolfur was out of his mind. Not that he wept or despaired; he may have done so the first few days, not after that. But he kept to himself, neglecting his wife and children as if they no longer concerned him. He seemed to feel that in losing his son he had lost everything. He bore his sorrow quite alone, never discussing it with anyone. No one sought to question him; no one dared attempt to console him; no one really saw him show any grief, until one winter when he began talking to himself.

Day and night, for a long time, he would talk to himself, always as though two or more persons were chatting, changing his voice to fit the different rôles, laughing and acting in every way as if engaged in a lively conversation. Everything he said was sensible, although it was often difficult to make out the subject under discussion. He would answer when addressed, slowly to be sure, but always good-naturedly and sensibly. There were often times when he seemed to have to wake himself up before he could answer. But while talking to himself, he always managed to get his work done as well as anyone who was wide awake.

He never talked about his son. These conversations were mostly about adventures he claimed to have experienced, some exaggerated, others entirely fictitious, or about this or that which he proposed to do sometime, or which he would have done, or ought to have done, never about anything in the present.

Rumors soon got about that Old Hrolfur was mentally unbalanced, and for a long time hardly anyone dared go to sea with him.

"But that fear has died out long ago," said Eirikur, smiling. "Now more would go if they had the chance."

"And does he have any luck fishing?"

"Luck seldom fails him."

"Then he must be pretty well off by this time?"

"I don't know. At least, he is not dependent on anyone, and he owns the fishing outfit himself."

"The old fellow lies on his money just like a dragon," said the man at the mast, wiping the spray off his face with his hand.

They then began telling me about Mula Island and the life in store for them the following week.

The island was a barren, desolate rock, out beyond the headlands. In autumn the surf covered it almost entirely. On reaching it, the first task before the fishermen was rebuilding the stone shelter of the year before, which had to be covered with rafters of driftwood and thatched with seaweed. That would provide them with a shelter at night in any weather. The landing place had been fashioned by nature herself; no work was required on that. But it was so treacherous that a man had to stand watch there constantly over the boats.

They would row out from the island with the bultow line every night and lay it on a certain bank. It was after midnight that the shark was greediest. Perceiving the fragrance of vilely stinking horse flesh and putrid seal blubber, he would then run on the scent and swallow everything placed before him. When he discovered the sad truth, that a huge fish hook with a strong barb was hidden within this excellent repast, and that it was not an easy matter to throw up the morsel again, he would try to gnaw the shank of the hook asunder with his teeth. Once in a while he accomplished this, but not often. Above the hook was a piece made of a heavy iron chain, which the shark sometimes could break more easily than the shank. When successful, this creature with the fine appetite, rejoicing in his regained liberty, would run on the next hook and be found there when the lines were pulled up.

If the shark failed in his attempt to cut himself loose, he would try to twist either the hook or the chain until it broke. But having foreseen this probability, man had so constructed the hook that it turned with the twist. With extraordinary patience, "the old gray fellow" would keep on twisting until he was pulled up to the gunwale and another hook had been thrust into him. Then he turned his ugly, sea-green, light-shy eyes on those who had done him this injury and began fighting with might and main, biting and thrashing about and almost capsizing the boat.

This method of fishing has been used by our forefathers from time immemorial. But now the shark is usually caught with decked vessels. In these parts no one except Old Hrolfur used this ancient method any longer.

He had caught many an "old gray fellow." Eirikur took one of the hooks from beneath the timbers and showed it to me. It was made of wrought iron, about half an inch thick, with a point of tempered steel. But it had been worn almost in two at the axis, and the shank was all bitten and gnawed. Many a time the "old gray fellow" had wrestled with it.

The fishermen told me so much about the fishing that I longed to go to the island with them.

All at once Eirikur nudged me.

We became silent and looked back to where Old Hrolfur sat in the boat.

"Now he has begun talking to himself."

We held our breath and listened.

Hrolfur sat motionless, holding the tiller lines. There was a far-away look in his eyes and a peculiar self-satisfied smile played on his face.

After a brief silence, he said, in a moderately loud voice:

"When I was on the frigate—"

That was all for the time being. His smile became more and more self-satisfied, as if an amusing adventure of his younger days were running through his mind.

"Yes, sir, when I was on the frigate—"

It was as if someone were sitting beside him, at the tiller, to whom he was telling the story.

"Has he ever been on a man-of-war?" I asked in a very low voice.

"Never in his life," replied Eirikur.

We gazed steadiy at Hrolfur. I still remember the twitching around his eyes. I could not see the eyes themselves, for the man looked as if he were asleep. But his forehead and temples were constantly in motion, as though in a pantomime.

I was silent. The world almost went black before me. Now it was perfectly clear that the man who held the tiller lines, the man who had our lives in his hands, was not in his right mind.

The fishermen nudged one another and grinned. They were accustomed to this.

"She would have foundered . . . would have been carried straight up on the rocks—hopelessly lost," said Hrolfur, "hopelessly lost, sir. She was a pretty craft, shiny black, with square white gun ports, ten guns on each side, and a carved figure at the prow. I believe the King would have been sorry to lose her. She was too pretty to be crushed to pieces, sir. They were glad when I came."

The fishermen suppressed their laughter with difficulty.

" 'Topsails up,' said I. 'Topsails up, sir.' He turned deathly pale, that gold-braided fellow. 'Topsails up, for the devil's sake,' said I. The bluecoats on the deck fell over one another in their frantic haste. Yes, sir, although I had no sword dangling at my hip, I said, 'Topsails up, for the devil's sake!' And they obeyed me. They obeyed me. They dared not do otherwise. 'Topsails up, for the devil's sake!' "

Clenching his fists around the tiller lines, Hrolfur half rose from the cross-beam.

Eirikur was bursting with laughter, but he tried to keep the old man from hearing him. The fishermen at the mast laughed more openly.

"She's passed!" said Hrolfur, nodding his head, a look of satisfaction on his face. "To sea! Straight out to sea! Let her heel over! It's good to have a little sea dash over her. Let the water seethe on the oarlocks, as we Icelanders say. What if she creaks a little! It merely proves that she is sound. While she creaks like that she can't be rotten. Oh, well, we'll sail the bottom out of her then, but forward she must go, forward, forward, forward she must go!"

Dropping his voice, Hrolfur dragged out the last few words.

By this time we were far out on the fjord. Because of the currents, the waves were getting larger and the sea more choppy. It had become very difficult to steer the boat well. But Old Hrolfur steered by instinct. Although he did not look up, he seemed to see everything about him. He seemed to sense the approach of the rollers which he had to steer ahead of or avoid. He veered very little from the main course. The boat slipped adroitly in among the waves, over them, ahead of them, or through them, as if it had human intelligence. The water never splashed over it; foaming and screaming the waves towered above it and rushed at it, but it somehow contrived to dodge them. It was as sensitive as a frightened hind, quick to respond to the rudder and smooth in every movement, like an eager, pacing thoroughbred. The spirit of Old Hrolfur governed it.

But Old Hrolfur himself was not there. He was "on the frigate." It was not his boat he was steeering at the moment, but a huge three-masted craft, with sails raking the skies and ten guns on each side, one of the miracles of human craftsmanship. The mainstays were of many-stranded steel wire; the halyards were twisted round each other, and beat against the masts and stays; they appeared to be badly entangled, yet were in perfect order, as free and straight as the nerves in the human body. No need to steer this huge vessel ahead of the waves or round them. On the contrary, she was allowed to attack them with her full weight, to grind them down and plough through them as though they were snowdrifts. Creaking and groaning, she plunged ahead over everything that came in her way, lay flat on her side before the wind, and left a long furrow in her wake. Above the bulwark of this huge craft Hrolfur's boat hung in two curved iron posts, like a tiny shell.

Once this dream had been in the far distant future. Now that there was no hope of its fulfillment, it was far in the past. Hrolfur *had* been "on the frigate."

For a long time Hrolfur talked to himself, telling how he had sailed the frigate safely to port and had been awarded the royal gold medal. We caught but a word of this rigamarole now and then, enough to get the thread of the story. Hrolfur talked Danish and Icelandic alternately; he changed his voice so as to impersonate several men. We could always infer from what he said where he was at the moment, whether he was addressing the seamen on the deck, or the officers on the quarter-deck, or whether, the deed accomplished, he was clinking glasses with them in the cabin.

The storm had abated somewhat, but because by this time we were so far out on the fjord, the waves were much larger. They were the tail-ends of the heavy seas raging outside, tail-ends that, despite the contrary wind, extended far into the fjord.

Hrolfur had stopped talking aloud and was now mumbling softly. A sort of peaceful drowsiness came over the fishermen near me, and I believe that for a while I almost fell asleep. Then, too, I must confess, I was not entirely free from seasickness.

Presently the man who had been sleeping in the space before the mast rose. He yawned several times, shook himself, and looked about him.

"Well, we'll soon be in the inlet," said he, needlessly talkative.

At this news I became wide awake and raised myself on one elbow. The mountain which I had seen from the village, then swathed in dark blue, now towered straight up above us, rocky and terrifying, with black sea-crags at its base. The crags were drenched with the spray from the breakers, and the booming in the basalt caves, as the breakers fell into them, was like the roar of a cannon.

"You can't possibly land in the inlet now, Hrolfur," said the fisherman, yawning again. "The surf's too heavy."

Hrolfur made as if he did not hear.

By this time we were all wide awake and looking towards land. I think the speaker was not the only one of us to shudder at the prospect of landing.

Suddenly in the mountain above us it was as if a screen were gently drawn aside, bringing the Mula Valley into view. A little later the gables of the farmhouses became visible. The houses stood on high ground and the shore was rocky.

The boat turned into the cove. There it was calmer than outside; the sea a little smoother.

"Let out the jib," shouted Hrolfur. It was Eirikur who obeyed this order and manned the sheet. Hrolfur let out the mainsail himself, at the same time holding the sheet. I interpreted this to mean that Hrolfur considered it safer not to have the sails fastened because of the frequent gusts of wind in the inlet.

"Are you going to sail into the inlet?" asked the fisherman who had been asleep. The words came through his nose, which was full of snuff.

"Shut up," said Hrolfur, in no gentle tone.

That man asked no more questions. In fact, none of us asked any questions. Now every instant was filled with suspense. In silence we all gazed at the crags, which were dripping with the white spray.

Wave after wave passed underneath the boat, raising it up high, as if to show us the surf. Then it would let us gently sink down into a trough and the surf would disappear, along with much of the shore itself. The wave had shut it out.

I thought it strange how slowly the boat moved, but I

soon had an explanation of that mystery. The boat, with everything in it, was still under the control of Old Hrolfur.

He let the wind out of the mainsail and kept the boat strangely motionless by turning the tiller back and forth. Standing before the cross-beam, he looked steadily towards the bow. He now no longer talked to himself. He no longer was "on the frigate," but in his own boat. He thoroughly realized the responsibility that rested upon him.

After waiting a while for an opening in the breakers, Hrolfur again sent the boat rushing full speed ahead.

Now the moment had come, the moment which neither I nor probably any of those who were with Hrolfur in the boat will ever forget. It was not fear that seized us, but rather something akin to an intense fever of expectation before a combat. If I had had my way then we would have turned back.

Standing motionless at the helm, Hrolfur looked alternately underneath the sail and to one side of it, chewing his quid hard and spitting vehemently. The twitching around his eyes was now less marked than earlier in the day. His calmness had a soothing effect on the rest of us.

As we approached the inlet, a large wave rose behind us. Eyeing it askance, Hrolfur spat scornfully and grinned. The wave rose higher and higher as it approached and reached us at the mouth of the inlet. By that time it had become so sharp as to be almost transparent at the top. It seemed about to break into the boat.

While I was still gazing at the wave, the boat suddenly seemed to sink down, as if all the water had been drawn from under her. It was the undertow; the wave was sucking the sea back. At the gunwale the bluish-green spray fell in cascades from the rocks in the mouth of the inlet. The boat almost stood on end, and the sea around it seemed to be boiling—in fact, it was boiling and had boiled the seaweed on the rocks into a thick, gruel-like mass.

Suddenly I felt as if an ice-cold whip had struck me on the cheek. Falling forward under the blow, I grasped the mainstay.

"Let go the jib," called Hrolfur.

When I looked up again, the sails were fluttering out beyond the sides of the boat, while the boat itself, filled with water to the thwarts, was gliding calmly and slowly up the inlet.

We were all quite safe and sound.

True, I felt the cold water trickling down my bare back, underneath my shirt, but that did me no harm. It was merely a kiss I had received from the youngest daughter of the sea queen Ran.

I looked at Old Hrolfur. His face was beaming with satisfaction. This feat was perhaps his greatest accomplishment; it was something few men could do.

The boat glided slowly up the calm waters of the inlet and came to a stop at the landing place, where two men from the farmhouse awaited us.

"Just as I said; it is Old Hrolfur," one of them called as we landed. "No one else could get into the inlet here in such a sea!"

Old Hrolfur merely lifted his eyebrows and grinned. He made no reply, but pulling the rudder off, so that it should not catch in the bottom, placed it across the stern.

We landed and dragged the boat part way up on the beach. How we welcomed the opportunity to stretch our legs after sitting and lying in cramped positions on the hard boards for almost four hours!

We were received with open arms by the farmers at Mula, and the things I requested for my journey were supplied as a matter of course. Nowhere does Icelandic hospitality flourish as in the outlying districts and remote valleys seldom visited by travellers.

Walking over to Old Hrolfur, who stood apart on the rocks, I thanked him for the passage and asked how much I owed him.

"How much you owe me?" asked Hrolfur, hardly glancing at me. "What the fare is? Just a moment, please, just a moment."

Hrolfur addressed me as he would an old friend, using the familiar *thou*, although we had never set eyes on each other before that day. On his face there was a frown. He was morose and curt, almost gruff, in his replies. Yet there was something attractive about him, something that awakened confidence and respect and made me like his familiarity.

"You want to know what the fare is? Let me think a moment."

His mind seemed to be elsewhere. He loosened his leather breeches, and reaching into the pocket of the patched rags he wore underneath them, drew out a large piece of chewing tobacco and took a bite. Then he broke off a small bit and threw it into the crown of his sou'-wester. This done, he fastened his breeches again, doing everything very deliberately.

"No doubt you got wet out there at the mouth of the inlet?"

"Oh, that was hardly worth mentioning."

"Sometimes it splashes disagreeably out there."

Hrolfur stood still, chewing his quid and staring at the mouth of the inlet. I thought he had entirely forgotten my question.

"Sometimes it splashes disagreeably out there," he repeated, emphasizing the words. I looked him straight in the face and saw that his eyes were filled with tears. Now the twitching was more pronounced, as it had been earlier in the day.

"There is many a boat has been swamped there," he added, "and some have gone no farther. But I have floated in and out successfully so far. Oh, well, 'The silver cup sinks into the sea, but the wooden bowl floats,' says the proverb. I once had to drag out of the inlet here him who was my better in every respect. Then I became acquainted with the old inlet."

He stood there a little longer, staring out over the inlet, but he remained silent. At last he wiped the tears away on the wrist of his mitten and seemed to come to himself.

"You were asking what the fare is, sir. It is nothing."

"Nothing? What nonsense!"

"Since you got wet, it is nothing," said Hrolfur smiling, although the tears still stood in his eyes. "It is an old custom among us that if the ferryman allows the passenger to get wet, even if only on his big toe, he forfeits all right to the fare."

I begged Hrolfur to accept something, but in vain. At last he became serious.

"The fare is nothing, as I've already told you. I have brought many a traveller here into the inlet, and have never accepted a single *eyrir*. But if sometime you should come to our village again when Old Hrolfur is at home, drop in at the Stifla and drink a cup of coffee with the old man—black coffee with some rock candy and a dash of brandy in it, if you'll do me the favor."

I promised to do that. And Hrolfur squeezed my hand firmly and emphatically at parting.

We three, the farmers of Mula and I, stood on the low flat rocks on shore, waiting to see Hrolfur and his crew pass the breakers.

The sailors had reefed the sails and taken their places at the oars, while Hrolfur stood before the cross-beam, grasping the tiller lines. They had not yet begun to row. Holding the oars up out of the water, they waited for a lull. Meanwhile, wave upon wave came rolling into the mouth of the inlet, each higher than the last, and broke with white foam over the rocks.

Hrolfur watched them steadily. With the utmost calm, he waited like a beast waiting to jump at its prey.

"All right, boys," said Hrolfur all at once. The oars struck the water with a resounding smack and the boat suddenly sprang forward.

Thus the Vikings of old probably rowed, thought I to myself.

The roar of the surf drowned out Hrolfur's words, but we felt certain he was urging his men to do their utmost. We saw them strain every nerve and the boat speed ahead.

At the mouth of the inlet the breaker rose to meet them, sharp and concave before it broke over the rocks. We held our breath. It was indeed a magnificent spectacle we were watching.

Hrolfur shouted some command. Instantly all oars were laid on the gunwale, like the fins of a salmon jumping a waterfall, and the boat plunged into the wave. For a moment we lost sight of it in the raging surf; only the mast was visible. When we saw it again, it was out beyond all the breakers. It had been going at a good speed and had been well steered.

Hrolfur then sat down on the beam as though nothing had happened, just as he sat earlier in the day when he was "on the frigate."

Two of the fishermen unreefed the sails, while the third began to bail out. Soon the boat was going full speed ahead.

I was overcome by emotion as I gazed after Old Hrolfur.

"Farewell, old hero of the sea!" thought I. "You would indeed deserve a beautiful frigate with which to cleave the waves around Iceland."

Tilting gracefully, the boat glided over the waves like a sea gull with outstretched wings. We stood still, watching it, until it disappeared round the headland.

Gudmundur Gudmundsson

GUDMUNDUR GUDMUNDSSON (1874–1919) was above anything else the sweet-voiced songbird among contemporary Icelandic writers, first and last a lyric poet, although he also wrote essays and articles for newspapers and periodicals. The very titles of some of his collections of poetry, such as *Strengleikar* (Melodies, 1903) and *Gígjan* (The Fiddle, 1906), are indicative of the inherent musical quality of his verse. Few Icelandic poets, past or present, have equalled him in mastery of delicate form and melodious language. He readily made new verse forms to suit his mood and theme and often succeeded excellently. On the other hand, he lacked originality and vigor. Many of his love poems, with a recurrent strain of underlying sadness, are among his best productions, as are likewise some of his nature poems, describing nature in her quieter moods, dreamy evenings and starlit nights, when stillness reigned on land and sea. Genuine religious feeling is an increasingly strong element in his later poems, though he had earlier shown his pronounced moral and religious bent with his cycle of poems *Ljósaskifti* (Twilight, 1913) on the introduction of Christianity to Iceland in the year 1000, and still more with his challenging series of poems entitled *Fridur á jördu* (Peace on Earth, 1911) the introductory poem of which is included here. Among his many translations into Icelandic, Tennyson's *Locksley Hall* may be specially mentioned.

PROLOGUE FROM "PEACE ON EARTH"

TRANSLATED BY JAKOBINA JOHNSON

LORD, God of peace, my spirit's high ideal,
To Thee I lift my hands in mute appeal,
Omnipotent, a miracle imploring.
Grant to my soul a vision of Thy light,
Charge Thou my song with Thy compelling might,
That it may rise—Thy peace on earth restoring.

Lord, God of love, unto my spirit show
In all their truth the depths of human woe,
Wherefrom the groans of multitudes are calling.
Mingled with tears they rise around Thy feet,
Beseeching looks of dying eyes entreat:
"Thy peace on earth, like dew on deserts falling."

Lord, God of wisdom, with prophetic fires
Cleanse Thou my soul, ennoble my desires,
Thy purpose to my lowly heart revealing.
Thy wonder-power of love in song and sound
Call from my harp in rhapsody profound,
The suffering and broken spirits healing.

Lord, God of peace, Thy beating heart impels
Mine own, when that with sweet compassion
swells,
Thy mercy for the sufferers imploring.
Wherefore I feel my spirit's wings grow strong
And courage rise to wake my harp in song.
O, may it rise—Thy peace on earth restoring.

LAMENT

TRANSLATED BY WATSON KIRKCONNELL

SNOWS cloaked
Mountain cliffs, and clinging
Frosts assailed the shore.
Seas smoked,
Heavy ice-floes flinging
With a muffled roar.
Storms stroked
The strand with buffets sore.
And we sat by the bright hearth singing
Of sunshine and love's sweet lore.

The sun rode
Ruddy to its pyre;
Touched the moors with red.
High glowed
The evening clouds, and higher
O'er the calm sea spread.
Gold strowed
Joy on the mountain's head.
But in by the dark hearth-fire
My hopes lay ashen and dead.

THE ROSE

TRANSLATED BY JAKOBINA JOHNSON

IT drooped and it faded, my rose of beauty rare.
The frost king raged madly.—

Then softly bent earthward its blossom sweet and fair,
And languished so sadly.
But God to His bosom the dying flower inclining,
Enwreathed in His glory the rose petals shining.
Sleep, dear one, in peace; in peace;
Unbroken peace.

Kristín Sigfúsdóttir

KRISTÍN SIGFÚSDÓTTIR (1876–   ), a farmer's wife in northern Iceland and the mother of five children, has nevertheless found time to write several volumes of fiction, as well as a successful play, *Tengdamamma* (Mother-in-law, 1923). Her first collection of short stories, on themes from the rural districts so familiar to her, was favorably received. She has ably interpreted Icelandic rural life in her novels *Gestir* (Guests, 1925) and *Gömul saga* (An Old Story, 1927–1928), especially in the first part of the latter. The second part, though showing unmistakable narrative talent and powers of observation, is somewhat lacking in concentration.

DESTITUTION

TRANSLATED BY MEKKIN SVEINSON PERKINS

THE church bells are calling the people to service.

Forceful and inviting, their message rings out into the stillness of the spring air. It touches the souls of men like a mysterious greeting from an invisible world. Century after century God has spoken to men through the ringing of the bells.

"Co-ome ye; co-ome ye. Leave ye riches; leave ye hunger; leave ye hatred; leave ye pride. Come ye, sisters; come ye, brethren. All are equal; all are equal."

And old and young, rich and poor, the people throng to the church doors. There is no class distinction in that throng. Men are going before the Almighty with their joys and hopes, with their sorrows and burdens, with their yearnings and prayers.

Today is confirmation day for many of the children.

The church is soon filled; every seat is taken. The organist begins the prelude; the murmur of voices ceases; the faces of the worshippers take on a Sabbath expression.

"Nearer my God to Thee," chants the choir. Hearts beat faster. The exaltation that placed this glorious anthem upon the lips of the author grips the hearts of men. "E'en though it be a cross that raiseth me," reechoes in many souls, and mighty waves of rapture fill the church as the hymn is sung.

Only a few give heed to the late comers, who walk slowly and silently, and huddle in the corners, so as not to disturb the service.

But now one of them, a woman, walks swiftly down the aisle without halting. As she passes, many stare, for she is so shabbily dressed. Both facial expression and movements bespeak such bewilderment that the eyes of all instinctively follow her as she wanders up and down the aisle.

She is looking for a seat, but no one rises to offer her one. Yet, as nearly everyone knows, she has not only walked a long way, but did much work before starting. The glances of some seem to say: "I wonder what that poor wretch can be doing in church?" Her whole appearance is so out of keeping with her surroundings that her presence makes everyone ill at ease, arousing in every breast feelings of vexation and resentment, tinged with sorrow.

Does she realize this? Her eyes fill with tears; her lips tremble; her mouth twitches as if she were about to burst out weeping. Then suddenly turning round, she walks out of the church. No one tries to stop her. This is Gunna the Pauper, a public charge, a woman unruly and ill-tempered, who has spent much of her life doing the most menial work for almost no pay.

No one even attempts to find out what became of Gunna the Pauper. The service goes on to its conclusion. Then follow congratulations, handshaking, loving words, rejoicing, and smiles.

The people begin streaming out of the church into the sunshine, to chat with friends and acquaintances and prepare for the journey homeward.

It is delightful to breathe the pure spring air after the stifling heat inside. The worshippers all feel extremely complacent in the consciousness of having attended divine service and having received its blessing. They all feel relieved and happy, as if their souls had been bathed in a refreshing spring.

While the church quickly empties, Gunna the Pauper, in her tattered rags, is seen standing in one of the corners. Her face is hidden in her handkerchief. Bitter sobs shake her. She seems utterly unaware of the throng streaming by, though many eyes turn in her direction and both sympathy and pity may be read in many glances. But no one speaks to her. Few things in this world so touch the heart as the sobs of those for whom there are no adequate words of comfort.

The people are going home from church. In groups, large and small, riding and walking, they pass down the highway. Those who have fine mounts, gallop ahead. Dust and sand are whirled up from the road, covering with a dense cloud all who walk close behind the horsemen.

When the first cavalcade has gone some distance, one of the riders sees a handkerchief lying near the edge of the road. He jumps down and picks it up. It is so soiled and unsightly that he is about to throw it away again but, suddenly changing his mind, places it in a saddle pocket. Then he rides on.

Soon after this the churchgoers see a woman coming towards them, running as fast as her legs will carry her and panting loudly. It is Gunna the Pauper. Everyone stops to stare at her. Why in the world should she be going back to the church at a breakneck speed? Her tattered shawl flaps loosely in the air like a pair of wings. Her torn skirt wraps itself around her ankles; at times it is pushed up to her knees and wound so tightly around her legs that she must halt briefly before she can proceed. Upon reaching the cavalcade, she stops short, breathless, unable to utter a word.

"You haven't found a handkerchief?" she pants at last.

So that was all. Because of that dirty ragged handkerchief, she had run as though racing for a prize.

Handing her the bit of linen, the man says: "We found this."

At sight of it, Gunna's face beams with pleasure and tears of joy spring to her eyes, already red with weeping.

"God be praised!" says she, as though relieved of a great anxiety. "The handkerchief is not mine. I borrowed it this morning and 'twould grieve me sore if I could not return it. You have done me a great favor. I'd have gone back all the way to the church to look for it. Thank you very much."

Her manner is so simple and sincere that no one dares

smile. Her whole happiness seems to depend upon the return of that handkerchief. Now, with words of farewell, she again sets out at a run.

The horses trot along the road. Gunna can keep up with them only for a while. She is soon quite breathless, her face red and sweaty.

"Must you hurry so?" asks one of the riders.

"Yes, yes, home to gather the ewes," she replies, panting.

The horses trot faster, as though striving to race with her, and she gradually falls behind. New cavalcades come up and gallop by. She falls farther and farther behind. At last she has become a mere shapeless figure once more and her shawl has turned into wings. On she runs, swinging both arms and clutching in her right hand the handkerchief for which she could not pay despite a lifetime of slavery, the handkerchief that had soaked up her tears of loneliness and despair.

One after another the groups of riders pass. At last Gunna has disappeared in a cloud of dust raised by the hoofs of thoroughbreds.

Jóhann Sigurjónsson

JÓHANN SIGURJÓNSSON (1880–1919), the farmer's son from northern Iceland, who is his country's greatest dramatist to date and whose reputation in that realm of letters even extends to America, also wrote lyric poems both in Icelandic and Danish. Several of these were printed in Icelandic periodicals, and a small volume of his Danish poems, *Smaadigte* (Verses), was published posthumously in 1920. This was only natural, when one recalls the rich lyric no less than dramatic qualities of his plays, so prominent for instance in his first published drama, *Dr. Rung* (1905). Lyric poetry was, in fact, his first love when he began writing in Icelandic, and the poetic similes which stud his dramas like sparkling diamonds are born of the same deep lyric strain in the author. Some of his lyric poems, such as "Bikarinn" (The Cup) and "Sorg" (Sorrow), are veritable masterpieces, and the latter is further noteworthy as one of the very first poems in free verse in Icelandic. "Greetings to Norway," which strikes a particularly timely note, as if written for today, shows, on the other hand, that the author was also a master of the ancient verse-form of Iceland, the historic Edda meter.

His play *Eyvind of the Hills*, published in English by the American-Scandinavian Foundation, has been produced by the Harvard Workshop Players and in New York.

A SONNET

TRANSLATED BY SKULI JOHNSON

SPRING has departed; early days' sweet scent
Has changed to summer's sultry pungency;
Our youth has gone, no dream-flecked galaxy
Decks the gray fields of days that are unspent.

We're born upon a headland bare and rent
By the dim-beaconed sea, Eternity!
With sweat and blood—such is man's history!
We've bought some shells, and lo, our lives are spent!

And yet I've ne'er loved more the day's dear sight.
—"Eternity" the lips of infants bear—
Before thee, Life, I bow on bended knees;
E'en as a shaded flow'ret looks for light
—The stalk can scarcely its own weight upbear—
With suppliant hands, thy shining rays I seize.

SORROW

TRANSLATED BY MAGNÚS Á. ÁRNASON

WOE, woe, unto the fallen city!
Where are thy streets,
Thy towers,
And thy sea of lights, the joy of night?
Like a coral in the bosom of the ocean
Thou dwelt beneath the blue sky.
Like a brooch of purest silver

Thou rested on the breasts of the earth.
Woe, woe!
Down in dark wells poisonous snakes are crawling,
But night takes pity on thy ruins.

The hoofs of life whirl dust into the sky—
Men in harness,
Insane women in golden chariots.
—Give me salt to eat, that my tongue be parched within my mouth
And silenced be my sorrow.

On white horses we rode into the blue arc of heaven
And played with golden spheres;
We hung on to the mane of darkness
While it plunged through the abyss of space;
And we slept like moonbeams on the ocean waves.
Where are the mountains that shall crumble over my sorrow,
Hills, that shall hide my nakedness with dust?
A red dragon flies through eternity's darkest night
And spews poison.
Sun after sun falls drop by drop
And bears new life, new sorrow.

GREETINGS TO NORWAY

TRANSLATED BY JAKOBINA JOHNSON

INTO Norway's
Open coastline

Sink the fjords
Fantastic carvings—
Scars that seam
The ancient visage
Of a warrior
Never vanquished.

Snowy white
Against the heavens
Towers the giant
Dovre mountain.
Fairness and wisdom
Upon his brow,
Alone—austere
He sits in judgment.

Backward I look
At times departed,
Across the threshold
Of a thousand years—
Lo, the broken shields,
Bloody weapons,
And shattered vessels
In Hafursfjord.

Sailed the vikings,
Shone the ornate
Dragon-heads,
O'er darkling waters.
Then gave Norway
To a new country

Boat-loads fair
   Of noblemen.

In new surroundings
   The kindred tree,
Changed in limb and bark
   And long-formed habits.
But the heart and core—
   Common language—
Unchanged remained,
   Through the ages long.

Therefore, shall all
   The sons of Iceland
Rejoice on Norway's
   Day of freedom.
As long as thoughts of spring
   Foster warm impulse,
And northern waters
   Break their icy bonds.

Unnur Benediktsdóttir (Hulda)

UNNUR BENEDIKTSDÓTTIR (1881–), better known as "Hulda," for she has always written under that pen-name, has enjoyed national recognition in Iceland for over thirty years, and forty years have passed since her first poems appeared in print. They soon struck a responsive chord in the hearts of her countrymen, especially by her revival of the time-honored rhapsodies (*thulur*), with which she has made a unique and lasting contribution to Icelandic literature.

"Hulda" grew up in a literary home environment, in the previously mentioned Thingeyjarsýsla in northeastern Iceland, where her father was librarian and a progressive cultural leader. Her rich and many-sided production, including no less than sixteen books of poetry, short stories, fairy tales, essays, sketches, and a full-length novel, is deeply rooted in her cultural background and testifies to her compelling creative urge, her poetic gifts, and not least to that love of beauty and purity of soul which are the fundamental characteristics of all her works. Her lyrics, which are comparable to those of such masters as Jónas Hallgrímsson and Gudmundur Gudmundsson, are her best work. Her latest book of poems (1933), a cycle of songs, constituting what may be called a spiritual autobiography, is written with tender feeling and delicate lyric charm. This lyric quality is present also in her prose and is the chief attraction of her two-volume novel *Dalafólk* (Valleyfolk, 1936 and 1939), a highly romantic description of rural life in Iceland.

IF THE MOONBEAM

TRANSLATED BY SKULI JOHNSON

If the moonbeam,
Airy and bright,
Feathers possessed
And the power of flight:
On his pinions of snow,
I would ask him to go,
O'er ocean and land
At my love's command.

If the moonbeam,
Tiny and bright,
Power possessed
That on words could alight:
On his pinions of snow,
I would ask him to go,
Across the wide air
My love-greetings to bear.

If the moonbeam,
Gentle and bright,
Features possessed
That would charm with their sight:
On his pinions of snow,
I would ask him to go,
And love's kiss impart
To the lad of my heart.

LILIES OF WHITE

TRANSLATED BY WATSON KIRKCONNELL

Lilies of white in a noon-day dream
Lift lashes of wondering eyes,
And breathe their scent at my window-sill
Like a lover's passionate sighs.

I sit and gaze at the summer light
In the violet heavens burning—
And think of an eye that is lit for me
With wonder and prayer and yearning.

THE WEDDING NIGHT

TRANSLATED BY MEKKIN SVEINSON PERKINS

The church bells were ringing.

Their sound, as bright and cheerful as could be produced by an old set of bells, was borne into the houses. Everyone smiled. Some went to the windows or the door and looked out. The prettiest girl in town was to be married that night. The young girls were all donning their best; they were going to the wedding. Servants kept rushing back and forth through the houses, ever in search of some needed article. At last, attired in all their finery, the girls came down to the parlor to mothers and grandmothers and, happy and carefree, left for the church. The older women shook their heads after the girls had departed. Yes, indeed, they knew life. Marriage could be a failure even though the bride were as lovely as a day in spring and the groom a fine fellow.

It was a bright July evening, the sky all blue and gold. As the village clock struck six, the bridal procession filed through the streets.

On the slope to the west of the village lay the cemetery, affording a fine view over the buildings and the fjord beyond. By a grave on which the grass was beginning to sprout a young man sat and watched the procession until it disappeared within the church, far in the south end of town. Long after the church doors had closed behind it, he stood there gazing at them.

Then turning round, he looked down at the grave and sighed softly.

He had had but one intimate friend, and that friend now rested there under the sod. He had loved but one woman, and she now knelt before the altar at another's side.

Though the sun warmed his neck and cheek, he was unaware of it. Though the fragrance of the birches from the glen was wafted to him by a soft breeze, he felt it not. He was communing with his friend: "To you alone I could have told it. You alone knew all."

He bent his head down upon the grass. It cooled his fevered brow, though the soil was parched by the sun. Perhaps it was merely imagination, but his thoughts seemed the calmer for it. He lay still, watching the procession of visions from bygone days.

In every one of them she appeared.

First as a light-footed little girl, in a short, red dress and a straw hat that would never stay on her head but fell down on her back, where, held by an elastic, it bobbed up and down on her loosely flowing tresses. It was delightful to see her run and to hear her laugh.

Then, a little older, she flashed by on a sled, her cheeks glowing in the cold.

Next he saw her walking serenely, clad in her confirmation dress, the loveliest among her companions. She had waited at the gate that day and looked in his direction as he passed by with his friend. He hardly dared extend congratulations; she seemed so grown-up, almost like a bride.

Then one night at a dance she had flown with him straight into the heaven of bliss. With her alone was happiness; all else was sadness. Later he learned the reason for her high spirits and her gayety: She had just learned that her dearest hopes were to come true. Thinking back on it, he remembered that she had been equally gay with everyone. But at first he had thought her smiles were meant for him alone.

Now a shadow darkened his reverie.

He was following his friend to the last resting place and she disappeared for the moment. On her return, she no longer was alone. A handsome young man walked at her side.

Last of all came the vision in the bridal veil. He looked searchingly into her eyes. "Don't you remember? Don't you remember? No one has loved you more than I." Her hair was spread out beneath the bridal veil; her lips were red; her arms lovelier than ever. She gave him a friendly smile and passed on. He could see the broad shoulders of the bridegroom at her side.

His sorrow crept out into every nerve. As he faced a

future without her, the cold and the darkness gripped him like an eclipse at midday.

Once again the church bells pealed out.

He rose to his feet and saw her come out of the church, white as a cloud in the summer sky, her husband like a shadow at her side. Slowly they approached. Now they were passing the cemetery. He could see the flowers in her bridal veil and her profile standing out above the grating in the gate. No one in the bridal party saw him. He was glad of that. No one must know where he was. No one must divine his thoughts. The procession was very long. Now and again the bride would disappear to the rear among the guests, but she always came back, looking white and pure as a dove. Everything seemed so strangely dark in contrast. Then she crossed the threshold of the man she loved, and finally disappeared, not to return.

In his mind's eye he could see a picture of her the next morning coming outdoors, lovely in her dignity as a wife, while he, poor unfortunate beggar, would stand afar off.

Once again the future opened out before him, a vast pitch-dark expanse, without sun or stars. The darkness weighed like a load upon his shoulders. He hid his face in the grave and wept.

The evening was far spent. Worn with violent weeping, he shivered in the chilly air. He leaned against the grave. The stones cast their black shadows behind them, while out beyond the shore stretched the dark blue sea. The dew was beginning to fall, softly, very softly. Up on the hill a plover still sang; it tripped along, halted, and then sang again so beautifully, its breast gleaming in the last rays of the setting sun. A gentle breeze ran along the ground, stirring every flower and every blade of grass, as though seeking to find out whether they had actually dropped off to sleep. Then it passed on, leaving a dead calm behind.

The eastern sky was bright, giving promise of a fine day. The blue haze that veiled everything in the east would later clear up and the first rays of light appear. Then would come the dawn, again lighting up the clouds with brilliant hues, and at last the sun itself would rise.

The young man in the cemetery stood up. He looked to the west, where the sun had set; then he ran his eyes to the north, out to sea; and finally brought them to rest on the blue in the eastern sky. In that soft, dark hue his spirit found peace. He was exhausted by the combat with stark reality which had held him so fast that he could not hear the voice of his heart.

Little did he realize that his thoughts were like the blue in the summer sky just before daybreak, which changes first to the brilliant hues of dawn and then gives way to a clear, bright day.

Jakob Thorarensen

JAKOB THORARENSEN (1886–) is a carpenter by trade, but carries on a literary tradition from both sides of his family. He has published five volumes of poems, which have established him as one of the outstanding Icelandic poets of the day. His poems are notable for their intellectual quality and for vigor in thought and expression. An outspoken realist, he is often bitterly satirical; nevertheless, it is not difficult to detect in his poems an undercurrent of genuine sympathy. He has written graphic descriptive poems and impressive historical pieces; he excells particularly in his narrative poems, which tell the life-story of various types of people and interpret their character.

It was, therefore, not surprising that he should also begin writing short stories, which he had been doing for a decade before publishing the first volume in 1929. With this collection he won a place in the forefront among Icelandic short story writers, a place which was made more secure when his second and third book of similar stories appeared in 1938 and 1939. Many of the stories are masterly in respect to close-knit plot-construction, effective characterization, and virile style. His relentless realism is similar to that of the poems, but here too beneath the surface, like a hidden fire, runs a strain of deep feeling.

DESERT DANGERS

TRANSLATED BY WATSON KIRKCONNELL

SOME awful Powers have been placed
Within the silence of the waste,

Adverse and alien to light and life.
They waken at the slightest sound.
Ah, rouse no echo from the ground!—
With one who calls they are at deadly strife.

They ask for silence and for peace,
And hate the murmuring release
Of chatter from a noisy human breast.
On their domain you must not fling
A button or a broken string—
They will not tolerate so rude a guest.

They rather find their happiness
In hideous northern blizzard's stress
When frosts are fierce and darkness reigns supreme.
Such deadly weather brings a ban
Against that puny plague called man,
Who nowhere in their wilds may then blaspheme.

To kill thee, friend, they ever seek
And hoard thy bones in deserts bleak,
Or wantonly thy carcass they despoil.
But he whom holy rites inter
Is proof against the pillager—
Their clutch is foiled by consecrated soil.

THE CATHEDRAL IN TRONDHEIM

TRANSLATED BY WATSON KIRKCONNELL

HERE silent art, yet wise and watchful-eyed,
Is smiling at a sea that gleams with fire.

Behold how holy truth and solemn pride
Shine radiantly from vaulted arch and spire!

The skill of masters, raised in reverent laud,
Is hewn in stone to voice the prayers of sense:
The mighty church itself says mass to God
Much better than a bishop's eloquence.

Herein are written runes of deathless worth—
The lessons to which ages will agree:
The culture, soul, and power of the North
Are blended in majestic trinity.

LAST WORDS

TRANSLATED BY MEKKIN SVEINSON PERKINS

JON STIGSSON, farmer at Midholt, lay at the point of death, and all was confusion in the *badstofa* itself, as well as in the passages, the pantry, and the kitchen. It was evening, almost milking time, and the hired girls were preparing to go out to the stable. But Jon took a turn for the worse, and it seemed evident that the end was at hand; therefore everything was at a standstill. It did not seem proper to start the milking until all was over. The hired girls kept wandering back and forth through the passages, whispering together about this engrossing event which, though it was both sad and pathetic, had, nevertheless, the excitement of novelty.

The mistress of the house had begun serving out portions of food in the pantry when one of the hired girls came flying out of the passage and informed her, in hushed pantomime, that the awful and fateful hour had arrived. Quickly wiping her hands on the corner of her apron, the mistress removed the cap from her head, and with it mopped the dust off her face. Then she hurried into the *badstofa.*

It was obvious that Jon was in great agony. It was also obvious that he wanted to tell his wife something, but for the moment the pain had the upper hand. Then the paroxysm passed, and he began to speak, but his words were indistinct and disconnected because of his weakness.

"Gudrun dear, our life together is about over. But the end has come sooner than I expected. I have so much to tell you before—so many things to ask you to forgive me, Gudrun."

"Don't say that, my love," said Gudrun. "You have just as much to forgive. That's always the case. People who live together are bound to fall out at times. But I can't imagine the Lord Almighty in His mercy and grace will be severe on the slight transgressions of His poor finite creatures."

"Oh, don't you believe it, Gudrun! They say He keeps a written record of all offenses and the like. There'll certainly be a long string against me! I'm very much afraid He'll find it hard to forgive much of my life, especially that I've so often used harsh words to you, my dear, when I've been angry."

"I won't listen to such talk," answered Gudrun. "On the contrary, now that this solemn hour has come, I can truthfully say that you've been kindness itself. Though, now and then, we've had a slight argument, it's not to be wondered at, especially as I've always given as good as

I've taken whenever we've had any words, and I trust the Lord will now forgive me."

At this Jon seemed to be much improved. He appeared less exhausted and took on a healthier look than he had worn for the last two or three days. Sitting half-way up in bed, he took the snuff horn from the corner of the table. It had lain there untouched ever since he became ill. He turned it over in his hands and seemed to be making preparations for taking a pinch.

"Then, too, I've sometimes been rather stingy with you, my dear, when it came to groceries and dry goods from the stores," he said. "Don't judge me too severely in that, or in other things. You've not been any more extravagant than other women, and not nearly so extravagant as your namesake of Margerdi."

Judging by all she saw and heard, Gudrun thought that, at least for the moment, there was no immediate danger of his dropping off, and so she considered there was less need for tenderness towards her husband and affectionate words. All her choicest and most endearing phrases were yet unspoken; she was saving them for the last—till the very end. Jon was showing real signs of improvement. He was once again interested in his snuff horn, and he cleared his throat with much vigor. And now that the conversation had turned to the subject of groceries, dry goods, and extravagance, she could not help expressing her mind.

"Yes, you're undoubtedly right there, my friend. Gudrun of Margerdi would not have sat quiet if she couldn't buy a handkerchief or a bit of linen from the store when she needed them, without her husband raising a fuss, or a pound of sugar, or a little coffee when a trip is made to the Spit. But that's one of the things I have sometimes had to put up with. Oh, well, it's no use bringing up all that. But I've often told you, Jon, that it doesn't pay to deprive the help of their afternoon coffee. That only breeds discontent and causes constant talk among the hired girls, and they don't get as much done as they otherwise would."

"What tommyrot!" said Jon, beating with his snuff horn on the side of the bed. "Coffee three times a day, with prices what they are! Meat brings something, of course, but wool and sheepskins sell much lower now than last year, and our debts keep mounting."

Gudrun's husband appeared to her to be almost entirely recovered. Now that his niggardliness, his everlasting, disgusting parsimony again reared its head and stabbed her with its piercing glance, she believed providence intended to permit them to live together much longer; and, of course, that was all for the best.

"Now, isn't that just like you, Jon! You'd never agree to any proposal of mine to add to the conveniences in this home unless you were much sicker than you are now. But let me tell you frankly that when the next trip is made to the Spit, I have to get seven ells of white linen, four and a half ells of the blue double-width goods, three spools of thread, and a few more trifles."

And now Jon's wife rattled on and on. She touched on numerous subjects, recalled many incidents of their long married life, and pointed out, with bold logic and pungent expressions, what a skinflint Jon had always been.

Gudrun was by nature an active and industrious woman. She could not sit with idle hands on the bed at her husband's side through a speech so inordinately long. First she made her own bed, which stood opposite Jon's, then she walked back and forth in the room, tidying this and that, moving spinning wheels and wool cards, putting everything in its place. At last she felt that something was wrong. Jon made no answer to her rebukes. He was always most stubborn, she knew, when he said nothing, and this drove her on to fresh utterance. The harsh words came thicker and faster; the infusion of logic grew less.

Twilight fell in the room and Gudrun was still too occupied to pay heed to Jon's condition. Then, happening to pass near his bed, she saw that he had dropped off to sleep.

She was startled. It was not normal slumber. She stepped to the head of the bed. Evidently the time had come for the kind, the affectionate words which Jon so well deserved, despite trifling faults which had marred their long married life. She laid her hand on his chest and nudged him gently.

"Jon, listen, Jon, my love! Really, you've always been a good and loving husband, a good manager, a kind father. You have been all that, Jon. And God knows I've returned all your love, Jon. Jon, do you hear me?"

But Jon did not hear. He had died about one minute after replacing the snuff horn on the corner of the table more than a quarter of an hour before.

THE ANSWER

TRANSLATED BY AXEL EYBERG AND JOHN WATKINS

THE girl Ingibjörg Thorgeirsdottir of Swanhill sat in the upstairs hall room on Easter Eve after the rest of the household had gone to bed. She had to answer the following letter, which she had received on Holy Thursday from beyond the mountain:

"Honored friend:

"Greetings and thanks for pleasant company. Well, Imba, so that's how it turned out. Do you remember what you said to me last winter when I mentioned you know what? You said you weren't thinking about men, you said, and shied away from it for dear life. But that's how it turned out just the same. And that's what I thought would happen as soon as I heard you had taken a job at Whitebrook.

"Well, there's no use crying over spilt milk. But what are you going to do now, Imba? For Sigvaldi's not much use. But now I would like to come to your rescue as if nothing had happened, if that's all right with you. And I'm hoping that with God's help we'll make a go of it, if we can get hold of a strip of land and God gives us life and health. And you won't need to worry about what's happened, you know. For that can happen to anybody and I don't suppose, if we once get together on a bit of land, it will be the last time for you. And as a matter of fact, old Eyolfur wants to retire now, so I have a half promise of

Myrarsel, if he does. In that case it would be best for us to get together right away this spring.

"I don't suppose you have much against me, Imba, even though you hesitated last winter. So you can think it over and let me know after the holidays.

"Sincerely yours,

"Jon Thordur Dathason"

She did not find this letter in the least like the one she had sometimes dreamed of in connection with the great day when she must obey that first sublime call of love, which would demand the unanimous response of mind and heart. No, this simple and outspoken letter was not like that. Nevertheless, it was magnanimous and in many ways peculiarly true and sincere. But there were at the same time thorns in this childish candor that stung her to the quick. "That's what I thought would happen as soon as I heard you had taken a job at Whitebrook," he wrote. The impudence of it! Who had given him the right to think anything at all either about her or her staying at Whitebrook?

She could still turn red with anger when she read this, but at the same time she had to admit to herself that pride was out of place under the circumstances. For this was nothing more than her foster-mother had also surmised when she said goodbye to her on the lawn in the spring with tearful admonitions and prayers, indeed with quite unreasonable admonitions, as it seemed to her then. As a matter of fact, she had gone to Whitebrook expressly—or at least partly—to wreak a furious revenge on Sigvaldi for his treatment of her cousin Lauga, who had suffered the same mishap there two years before. Although of course there was really no comparison, for Lauga was frivolous.

Was Lauga frivolous? But what about herself then? Oh, how she prayed God to forgive all her pride and uncharitableness!

As it happened, she and Lauga were third cousins. And she longed exceedingly to avenge this cousin of hers, who was now struggling along in the West country, bound and branded, penniless and despised. "For Sigvaldi's not much use," as he wrote in the letter. Obviously it was true, but still she considered it impudence to say such things. It was nobody's business.

Yes, she had been at Whitebrook . . .

And now—now, when everything was over and done with and everything too late, it seemed to her that she might have come out of it better if she had not armed herself with such violent hostility towards Sigvaldi, as was actually the case during the first few weeks she had lived there.

He had in all probability seen right through her at a glance, had shrewdly taken her measure, and concluded that he had only to use more skill, to dig a little longer and a trifle deeper for her favor than for some of the other girls'.

Her hostility had doubtless been far too obvious in the beginning. He parried with silence, so that there was about all his behavior a curious air of resentment. To be sure he observed all the courtesies; but when he told her what to do, his orders were curt and dry. Then he usually swung off, leaving her alone at work with the hired man—all through the harvest, you might say.

And yet she had felt it in her bones right from the start that this would happen, that it must happen some time sooner or later. And she was almost consumed with vindictive impatience to humiliate him—almost to spit in his face when he should come, both for her cousin Lauga's sake and for the sake of her own honor.

But not a move did he make.

As the harvest went on, however, his attitude gradually changed. Sigvaldi became more affable. She was a quick, smart girl at the haying—as he could not fail to notice. And that, of course, may well have had something to do with the change in his attitude. But at the same time she felt quite sure that "this" was now drawing near.

When it was good drying weather, he might take a notion to send the hired man home to tend hay near the barn and would stay alone with her working at the hay up in the mountain. And then she was certainly on her guard, especially when they sat down to eat or drink coffee.

But his conduct was irreproachable and astonishingly circumspect, as before. His conversation, too, was very dignified and serious, with just a sprinkling of fun, as though for spice, at the proper time.

It was sometimes quite dusky when they walked home from the fields; but that made no difference. He trudged along at her side and kept on talking about this and that. It could hardly be called conversation—on account of her suppressed excitement she was often unable to answer more than a word here and there far apart. But he never made a move. And so it went on week after week.

Finally she got to the point where she really ceased to understand it at all. Had he been falsely accused? Had he been pursued by those infallible rumors which, the proverb says, seldom lie?

Or—or was *she* not as good-looking as her cousin Lauga, was she really not as good-looking? Had she not, for example, a distinctly more slender figure? Or didn't she blush just as becomingly?

Of course it was nothing but natural that he should make considerable demands in these respects, for he was a fine figure of a man. Yes, the recognition of this had struck root in her mind the very first week at Whitebrook. And as time passed, her conviction of this became so strong that she was half dissatisfied with his wife—dissatisfied for his sake, for whatever his faults it was impossible to deny that he was a fine figure of a man.

But "the mind alone knows what lies in the heart." Perhaps he had some burden to bear; his caution and seriousness pointed in that direction—and strange to relate, before she was aware of it herself, she had begun to make excuses for him in various ways in her own mind and had started to spread a kind of veil of sympathy over this great sin of his, for which she had resolved to punish him whenever the opportunity offered.

She did not realize then nor until long after that all this was the result of his skill in preparing the ground in matters of this kind—she went about completely unaware that she herself was ripening on this perilous soil and becoming, so to speak, ready for harvest.

No, about this time she knew only that when he had finished shaving on Sunday mornings, his chin had hardly its equal in the whole wide world. And occasionally their eyes met, but that was not allowed, and they immediately looked away again.

One Sunday, just before the end of the haying season, he came home from a vestry meeting late in the afternoon. He greeted the people in the house curtly, walked straight through the living room, and disappeared into the connubial bedroom, but as often happened, he left the door ajar. She saw him sit down at the table in front of the gable window and begin to look through the pages of the parliamentary record. She remembered this as clearly as if it had happened today.

Out in the living room there were three people: she herself, sitting on her bed patching her blue blouse, old Thorhildur Pálsdottir swaying back and forth, as very old women do, on the edge of the bed, and knitting a new foot on an old stocking, and finally the handyman, lying flat on his belly in his bed, overcome by the sloth and dullness of the day of rest.

The mistress was busy outside. She was very sloppily dressed as usual, and somehow not nearly attractive enough for such a handsome husband—as it seemed to her. But then she had of course become a prey to sinful thoughts and was not on her guard.

In a little while the separator started out in the pantry, and now the mistress would certainly have her hands full for the next half hour. And just at that moment the master put down the parliamentary records and peered around him.

"Ingibjörg, would you mind pulling off my boots?" he called out to her.

She got up at once and disappeared into the gable room.

"Close the door after you, my dear," he said in a low voice.

She obeyed, of course, and the door was immediately closed.

That's all there was to it, not another word. But now it had happened after all—now it had happened. What a mad thing to do! And yet it was built on a remarkably firm foundation and in reality rested on four stout pillars: in the first place on her own ripeness, in the second place on the advanced age and slowness of old Thorhildur, in the third place on the exceeding sloth of the handyman, and last but not least on the steady hum of the separator from the pantry.

She had always intended to leave Whitebrook about sheep-gathering time. But she did not go away until much later, not until the home was ablaze with the flames of strife, in the same way as when her cousin Lauga was given her walking ticket two years before. The stream of life is sometimes turbid when it strays from its proper course.

Never again could she set foot in that house. Nor could she make her home at Swanhill in the future either, for her foster-mother's eyes were wet with tears all day long and old Thorleifur was raging mad at the underhand tricks of the flesh and the world. It wouldn't surprise her at all, if he—although he had really gone to bed—should soon poke his head up through the attic door and hurl at her some sort of gibes or taunts.

And therefore it was of course best that she hasten to answer the noble offer contained in this letter of Jon Thordur

Dathason's, who was a rather simple-minded, freckle-faced hired man on a farm called Hjallar, on the other side of the mountain. She knew that he was an honest, hard-working, and capable man, although he did not bear much resemblance to the glamorous heroes of certain sparkling love stories. For a little while she stared out into the blue and pondered on the enigma of life and the guidance of God. But then the pen got busy:

"Honored and dear friend:

"I received your letter on Holy Thursday, for which I thank you, and yet I am somewhat at a loss how to answer it. There is so much in this letter of yours that does not please me, and yet I know that no harm is intended, although some things might appear that way as they are written in your letter. It seems rather unnecessary to me that you should have to make that remark about Sigvaldi's not being much use. Do you think you need to remind me that he is tied up and not free to do as he would like? And although things went as they did with us, he is still a charming person. Oh, Nonni, I can never forget him and I can't bear to hear anyone reproach him.

"As far as Myrarsel is concerned, I would not want you to lose the opportunity on my account, if you can rent the place and are satisfied with me as I am. And although I have made a misstep, I want to make you a good wife just the same. You need only one pack horse, for you can put my chest of drawers in one pack and my little box, comforter, and pillow in the other. Burn this letter.

"Yours sincerely,

"Ingibjörg Thorgeirsdottir."

She glanced over the letter and saw at once that it badly needed to be rewritten, especially the first paragraph—where her heart was revealed. But at this moment she heard a rustling noise in the hall and hurried to close the letter.

And she was just in time. Old Thorleifur poked his head up through the opening.

"What the devil are you dawdling about here for, Imba? Go straight to bed," he said. "Don't you think you are burden enough in the house without keeping us awake into the bargain?"

Awake? Yes, it's true, of course, that suspicion never sleeps. There was nothing more likely than that Old Thorleifur would think she was like a drunkard who keeps on and on. But there was certainly no dangerous company here in the attic, she thought, among the harness, hooks, ropes, and junk.

But on account of her foster-mother she did not answer the old man but followed him silently in through the hall. And she held her fate in her hand sealed in a gray envelope.

Jakob Jóhannesson Smári

JAKOB JÓHANNESSON SMÁRI (1889–   ) studied Scandinavian philology at the University of Copenhagen and has for many years taught Icelandic language and literature in the State College of Iceland at Reykjavík; besides teaching he has written a large number of essays, book reviews, and other works in prose. His main contribution is, however, in the field of creative literature, and he has to his credit three books of original poetry. His poems are characterized by fine lyric quality and deep spirituality. He has written numerous nature poems and is a master-painter in words; his poems are as a whole unusually polished in both vocabulary and metrical form, and it is indicative of his mastery of form that he has written numerous excellent sonnets. He is not as vigorous a poet as many of his countrymen. Rather, he is a mystic, endowed with uncommon insight and all-embracing sympathy. He has proved himself a productive and able translator of both prose and verse; included among his translations is Kipling's famous "If."

THE HARP

TRANSLATED BY WATSON KIRKCONNELL

SOMETIMES a still small voice of music steals
Across the ocean's din, the desert's hush,
The fragrant dreams of opening flowers—
But most when night my spirit seals.

Half-forgotten tales then rush
Across the mind's blue stream of misty hours.

Over life's cold expanse of snowy miles
 A sleeping infant smiles.
It breathes—and the heart beats under
Those violet strains of wonder
Possessing my soul.

But up in the dark gulfs yonder
The ice-blue star-flames roll.

Davíd Stefánsson

DAVÍD STEFÁNSSON (1895–   ) is an unusually productive writer, six large volumes of poetry having already appeared from his pen, besides a novel and two dramas. With his first book of poems, *Svartar fjadrir* (Black Feathers, 1919) he immediately became a great favorite with the Icelandic reading public and still retains his firm hold on it. Unquestionably, he is the most popular of contemporary Icelandic poets as far as the nation at large is concerned. With his lightness of touch and the musical quality of his poems, as well as with the selection of his themes, he struck a new note in modern Icelandic poetry. Naturalness and simplicity in vocabulary and meter are among his attractive qualities, together with vividness of description and variety of mood. Whether he writes on Icelandic or non-Icelandic themes, whether he seeks his subject matter in external nature or the lives of individuals, or deals with social questions, there is about his poems a vivacity and spontaneity characteristic of the true lyrist.

With his first novel, a two-volume serial, *Sólon Islandus* (1940), remarkable alike for its poetic style, narrative skill, and profound psychological insight, he has won new admirers and added to his stature as a writer. His reputation has also been enhanced by his new, brilliantly conceived and constructed play, *Gullna hlidid* (The Golden Gate, 1941), built around a theme from Icelandic folklore.

ABBA-LABBA-LÁ

TRANSLATED BY SKULI JOHNSON

I

HER name was Abba-labba-lá,
She was dark of cheek and brow,
  And her cabin in the wood
'Neath the green-grown branches stood;
With faith in stocks and stones indued
  Was Abba-labba-lá.

II

And no one knew from what place
  She came into this wood;
And none knew for what reason
  She played in madcap mood;
And why she struck and bit—that
  No mortal understood.

III

Her name was Abba-labba-lá,
She was dark of cheek and brow,
And all who sought to win her
  She maddened—none knew how.
By the blood of wild beasts,
By the blood of wild beasts,
  Lived Abba-labba-lá.

IV

. . . At one time beheld I
  Abba-labba-lá.

She danced within the forest,
Dark of cheek and brow.
Loudly her I hailed then—
My heart was touched, I trow—
"Abba-labba,
Abba-labba,
Abba-labba-lá!"

V

She kissed me and laughed when
She'd come to my side,
Then bit me and sucked all
My blood—so I died.

VI

O'er sea and land now shout I,
A specter from the howe:
"Beware, poor mortals,
Beware, poor mortals,
Of Abba-labba-lá!"

I SAIL IN THE FALL

TRANSLATED BY WATSON KIRKCONNELL

I

SUMMER is dying, is dying,
And cold is the breath of fall.
The waves are beginning to labor
And beat on the ocean-wall.
The leaves are blown from the branches.

The children have frost-reddened lips.
The birds are departing. Keen strain at
their cables
The storm-hearted ships.
I yield to a mighty power.
I am drawn by a hidden hand.
And the sea—the sea is calling
In tones I cannot withstand.
I am the bird that passes,
The ship that the tempests blow.
My song is a song of parting.
I came, and I go.

II

The storm leads away from harbor.
Surf beats the ocean-wall.
I came from the south in summer
And sail in the fall.
Prayers cannot hope to hold me.
I hack through the holiest ties—
Abandon the woman I worship,
The land of my boyhood skies.
I turn from the ship a moment
To speak the farewells I owe.
But my song is a song of parting.
I came, and I go.

III

I envy all that can scorn thee,
Thou wave-driving wind of the deep!—
The sun that glitters in glory,

And the lands that lie asleep;
The peaks in their crystal beauty,
Silent and heaven-high;
And the sphinx that keeps its secret
While the myriad years go by.

IV

I am borne by breeze and billow
From land on to land.
I ask not the people for praises
Or honoring hand.
I long to be blest with friendship,
But am everywhere ever alone,
Ever a man without country,
A vagrant in every zone.
But my song is a song of parting.
Surf beats the ocean-wall.
I came from the south in summer
And sail in the fall.

Gudmundur Gíslason Hagalín

GUDMUNDUR GÍSLASON HAGALÍN (1898–   ) has gained a place among contemporary prose writers of Iceland, alike with his excellent short stories and his novels. He is the author of a number of volumes of short stories of everyday life, especially the life of the Icelandic fishermen, which he knows from his own experience and from close association with the men of the sea. In several of the more recent of these stories he brings out in a subtle fashion the fundamental part which illusion plays in human life; here his humor, which runs from good-natured comedy to pure burlesque, is also much in evidence.

Of his novels, *Kristrún í Hamravík* (1933) is notable both for style and cultural importance. This is to an even greater degree true of his major work in the realm of fiction, the two-volume novel *Sturla í Vogum* (1938), unquestionably his richest book. Everything is here conceived on a grander scale than in his earlier works, and the hero, Sturla, is a rugged individual, obviously a man after the author's own heart. During the last few years Hagalín has also written two significant biographies, one of an old shark-fisherman and one of an adventurous skipper, based on their own narratives. The heroic and national element is strong in both these books and they are a real contribution to the cultural history of modern Iceland. This is especially true of the second, *Saga Eldeyjar-Hjalta* (1939), which is indeed a modern saga.

THE FOX SKIN

TRANSLATED BY MEKKIN SVEINSON PERKINS

"No need to take care now about fastening the door," Arni of Bali said to himself as he wrapped the string around the nail driven into the door-post of the outlying sheepcote. Then he turned round, took out his handkerchief, and, putting it to his nose, blew vigorously. This done, he folded the handkerchief together again, wiped his mouth and nose, and took out his snuff horn.

What fine balmy weather, thought Arni. That miserable fox won't come near sheepcotes or houses now. Blast its hide! Yes, it has caused him many a wakeful night. All the neighboring farmers would have the fool's luck to catch a fox every single winter. All but him. He couldn't even wound a vixen, and had in all his life never caught any kind of fox. Wouldn't it be fun to bring home a dark brown pelt, one with fine overhair? Yes, wouldn't that be fun? Arni shook his head in delight, cleared his throat vigorously, and took a pinch of snuff.

Bending his steps homeward, he trotted along with his body half stooped, as was his habit, and his hands behind his back. When he looked up, he did not straighten out, but bent his neck back so his head lay between his shoulder blades. Then his red-rimmed eyes looked as if they were about to pop out of his head, his dark red beard rose up as though striving to free itself from its roots, and his empurpled nose and scarlet cheek-bones protruded.

Pretty good under foot, thought Arni. At least it was easy to go between the sheepcotes and the house. Everything pretty quiet just now. The sheep took care of themselves during the day and grazing was plentiful along the seashore and on the hillsides. No reason why he might not now and then lie in wait somewhat into the night in the hope of catching a fox; he wasn't too tired for that. But he had given up all that sort of thing. It brought only vexation and trouble. Besides, he had told everybody that he did not think it worth his while to waste time on such things and perhaps catch his death to boot. The Lord knew that was mere pretense. Eighty crowns for a beautiful dark brown fox skin was a tidy sum! But a man had to think up something to say for himself, the way they all harped on fox-hunting: "Bjarni of Fell caught a white vixen night before last," or "Einar of Brekka caught a brown dog-fox yesterday." Or if a man stepped over to a neighbor's for a moment: "Any hunting? Anyone shot a fox? Our Gisli here caught a grayish brown one last evening." Such incessant twaddle!

Arni's breath came short. Wasn't it enough if a man made an honest living? Yet work or achievement which brought no joy was unblessed. At this point Samur darted up. Arni thought the dog had deserted him and rushed off home. Now, what in the world ailed the creature? "Shame on you for a pesky cur! Can't you be still a minute, you brute? Must I beat you?" asked Arni, making threatening gestures at Samur, a large, black-spotted dog with ugly, shaggy hair. But Samur darted away, ran off whimpering; he would pause now and then and look back at his master, until finally he disappeared behind a big boulder.

"What's got into the beast? He can't have found a fox trail, can he?"

Arni walked straight to the rock where Samur had disappeared; then slowing down his pace, he tiptoed as if he expected to find a fox hidden there. Yes, there was Samur. There he lay in front of a hole, whimpering and wagging his tail.

"Shame on you, Samur!"

Arni lay down prone on the snow and stretched his arm into the hole. But all of a sudden he jerked his hand back, his heart beating as if it would tear itself out of his breast. He had so plainly felt something furry inside the hole, and he was badly mistaken if a strong fox odor did not come out of it. Was the fox alive, or was it dead? Might it bite him fatally? But that made no difference. Now that he had a good chance of taking a fox, it was do or die. He stood up straight and stretched every muscle, and pulled the mitten on his right hand carefully up over his wrist. Then he knelt down, thrust his hand in the hole, set his teeth, and screwed up his face. Yes, now he had caught hold of it and was pulling it carefully out. Well, well, well, well! Not so bad! A dark brown tail, a glossy body, and what fine overhair! For once Arni of Bali had some luck! The fox was dead; it had been shot in the belly and just crept in there to die. Sly devil! Poor beast! Blessed creature! Arni ended up by feeling quite tenderly towards the fox. He hardly knew how to give utterance to his joy.

"Good old Samur, my own precious dog, let me pat you," said Arni, rubbing the dog's cheek with his own. They could shout themselves blue in the face. It was no trick to kill all you wanted of these little devils if you just had the powder and shot and were willing to waste your time on it. But here Arni's face fell. He did not even have his gun with him. It stood, all covered with rust, at home out in the shed. Just his luck! And how could he claim to have shot a fox without any gun? "Get out of here, Samur. Shame on you, you rascal!" And Arni booted Samur so hard that the dog yelped.

But in direst need help is at hand. He could wait for the cover of darkness. Not even his wife should know but that he had shot the fox. Wouldn't she stare at him? She had always defied him and tried to belittle him. No, she should not learn the truth, she least of all. He would not tell a soul. Now Samur, he knew how to hold his tongue, faithful creature! Arni sat down on the rock, with the fox on his knees, and started singing to pass the time, allowing his good cheer to ring out as far as his voice would carry:

My fine Sunday cap has been carried away
By a furious gale;
And I'll wear it no more to the chapel to pray
In the wind and the hail.

He chanted this ballad over and over again until he was tired, then sat still, smiling and stroking the fox skin. He had learned the song when he was a child from his mother, who had sung it all day long one spring while she was shearing the sheep. And he could not think of any other for the moment. It wasn't, in fact, a bad song. There were many good rhymesters in Iceland. He began singing again, rocking his body back and forth vehemently, and stroking the fox skin the while. And Samur, who sat in front of him, cocked his head first on one side, then on the other, and gave him a knowing look. At last the dog stretched out his neck, raised his muzzle into the air and howled, using every variation of key known to him. At this Arni stopped short and stared at him, then bending his head slightly to one side to study him, he roared with laughter.

"What an extraordinary dog! Yes, really extraordinary!"

In the little kitchen at Bali, Groa, the mistress, crouched before the stove and poked the fire with such vigor that both ashes and embers flew out on the floor. She was preparing to heat a mouthful of porridge for supper for her old man and the brats. She stood up, rubbed her eyes and swore. The horrid smoke that always came from that rattletrap of a stove! And that wretched old fool of a husband was not man enough to fix it! Oh, no, he wasn't handy enough for that; he went at every blessed thing as if his fingers were all thumbs. And where could he be loafing tonight? Not home yet! Serve him right if she locked the house and allowed him to stay in the sheepcotes, or wherever it was he was dawdling. There now, those infernal brats were at the spinning wheel. Groa jumped up, darted into the passage, and went to the stairs.

"Will you leave that spinning wheel be, you young devils? If you break the flier or the upright, your little old mother will be after you."

A dead calm ensued. So Groa returned to the kitchen, and taking a loaf of pot-bread from the cupboard, cut a few slices and spread them with *braeding*.*

* A mixture of tallow and cod liver oil or whale oil.

Now a scratching sound was heard at the door, and Arni entered.

"Good evening to all," said he with urbanity, as he set down the gun behind the kitchen door. "Here's that gun. It has certainly paid for itself, poor old thing."

His wife did not reply to his greeting, but she eyed him askance with a look that was anything but loving.

"Been fooling around with that gun! Why the blazes couldn't you have come home and brought me a bit of peat from the pit? A fine hunter you are! I might as well have married the devil." And his wife turned from him with a sneer.

"You're in a nice temper now, my dear. But just take a look at this," said Arni, throwing down the brown fox on the kitchen floor.

At first Groa stared at her husband as if she had never seen him before. Then she shook her head and smiled sarcastically.

"You found it dead, I'll wager!"

Arni started. His face turned red and his eyes protruded.

"You would say that! You don't let me forget what a superior woman I married! Found it dead!" And Arni plumped down on the wood-box.

His wife laughed.

"I'll wager I hit the nail on the head that time!"

Arni jumped to his feet. That confounded old witch should not spoil his pleasure.

"You're as stark, raving mad as you always have been. But I don't care what you say. Kids, come and look at the fox your father has shot."

Three days later they had a visitor. Arni stood outside and stared at him. For a wonder, somebody had at last found his way to Arni's. Days and nights had passed but nobody had come. They always came when they weren't wanted. And now came Jon of Lon, that overbearing fellow! But now he could see that Arni of Bali was also a man among men.

"Howdy, Arni, you poor fish!" said Jon, fixing his steely gray eyes on Arni.

"How are you, you old snake!" answered Arni, smiling contemptuously. What monstrous eyes Jon had when he looked at a person!

"Has something special happened? You're somehow so puffed up today," said Jon, with a sarcastic smile.

"Darn him!" muttered Arni. Was he going to act just like Groa? In that case, Arni had at least a trump card in reserve.

"Did you say something?" inquired Jon, sticking a quid of tobacco into his mouth. "Or wasn't it meant for my ears? Oh, well, I don't care for your mutterings, you poor wretch. But now go ask your wife to give me a little drink of sour whey."

Arni turned round slowly and lazily. Wasn't the old fellow going to notice the skin? It wasn't so small that it couldn't be seen. There it hung on the wall, right in the sunlight, combed and beautifully glossy.

"That's quite a nice fox skin. Whose is it?" asked Jon, walking over to the wall.

Arni turned round. He could feel his heart beating fast.

"Mine," he said, with what calm he could muster.

"What's the idea of you buying a fox skin, you poor beggar?"

"Buying?" Arni sighed. "You think I can't shoot me a fox?"

"You!" Jon laughed. "That's a downright lie, my dear Arni."

"A lie! You'd best not tell people they lie unless you know more about it. A scoundrel like you, I say, a scoundrel like you!" replied Arni, swelling. "I think you'd better be getting in and see her. You know her pretty well, I believe."

Jon looked at the farmer of Bali with his steely eyes.

"For whom are you keeping the skin, Arni?"

"No one," said Arni crossly; then after some hesitation, "The Lord gave it to me."

"All right, Arni. Miracles never cease. That is plain enough after this, and no question about it. That's an eighty-crown skin, however you came by it. But now let's go in and see Groa. As you say, I know her pretty well. She was a smart girl, you poor wretch. Too bad I was married and had to throw her to a creature like you."

Arni grinned and, trotting to the door of the house, called: "Groa, a visitor to see you."

The woman came to the door. A smile played about her lips, smoldering embers glowed in her blue eyes, and the sunlight lighted up the unkempt braids of golden hair which fell down about her pale cheeks.

But Arni for once was satisfied. At last Jon was properly impressed. The affair between Groa and Jon was something that could not be helped. Jon surely regretted having lost that girl! Yes, indeed! And she had her good points. She was smart, and a hundred crowns a year, besides everything else that was brought them from Lon, was pretty good compensation. Yes, many a man had married less well than Arni of Bali. And the children were his, most of them, anyway. Nobody need tell him anything else.

The fox skin became Arni of Bali's most cherished possession. Every day, when the weather was clear, he would hang it, well smoothed and combed, on the outside wall, and when he left home he carefully put it away in a safe place. The skin became famous throughout the district, and many of the younger men made special trips to Bali to examine it. Arni would beam with joy and strut around with a knowing, self-satisfied expression on his face, and would tell of the patience, the agility, and the marksmanship he had to put into killing this monstrously clever fox. It certainly wasn't hard to kill all you wanted of these devils, if you just had the powder and shot and were willing to give your time to it, he would say, as he turned the skin so that the sunlight shone full on the glossy pelt.

Then one day that fall, Arni came home from tending the sheep, which had just been brought down from the mountain pastures. He hung the skin out and went into the kitchen, where Groa was busy washing, sat down on a box by the wall on the other side of the room, let his head rest on his hands, and looked wise. For a while there was silence. At last Groa looked up from her washtub and gave Arni a piercing glance.

"Have you got your eye on a cow to replace the gray-spotted one we killed last spring?"

"Cow?" asked Arni, scratching his head. "Cow? Yes, so you say, my good woman."

"So I say? Do you think the milk from Dumba alone goes very far in feeding such a flock of children as we have? You haven't gone and squandered the money we got for Skjalda?" asked Groa, looking harder still at her husband.

"Don't be foolish, woman! The money lies untouched at the factor's. But he wouldn't pay much for the meat and hide of Skjalda, not anywhere near enough to buy a good milch cow. He said the English on the trawlers don't set much store by cow's meat. The summer has been only so-so, and I'm sure we'll have plenty of uses for what money I've been able to scrape together. Of course, a cow is a good thing to buy, an enjoyable luxury, if only you have the money."

"If you can't scrape together the money for a cow, we must cut expenses somehow. Perhaps you could stop stuffing your nostrils with that dirty snuff? And you ought at any rate to be able to sell that fancy fox skin you play with so childishly."

"Is that so!"

"Yes, you play with that wretched fox skin just exactly like any crazy youngster."

"Wretched is it? Take care what you say, woman! Wretched skin! A fine judge of such matters you are!" And standing up, Arni paced the kitchen floor. "An eighty-crown skin! And you call that wretched! Jon of Lon didn't call it any names. You'll believe at least what he says."

"Now, don't get puffed up. You ought to be thankful

to get what you can for the skin. It will help in buying the cow."

"The cow? Let me tell you, woman, that I am not going to buy a cow for the skin. You can take it from me that you will never get a cow for that skin. Or anything else, in fact. The farmer at Lon can shell out whatever is needed for buying the cow. That's the least he can do for you."

Groa stopped her washing, stared for a few seconds at Arni, and then with a quick movement walked up to him, brandishing a bit of wet linen.

"Will you tell me what you're going to do with the skin?" she asked, almost in a whisper.

Arni shrank back. The way to the door was cut off. He raised his arm in self-defense and retreated as far as possible into the corner.

"I'm going to sell it. Now be reasonable, Groa. I'm going to sell it."

"And what are you going to buy for it?" his wife hissed, boring into him with her eyes.

"A cow. I'm going to buy a cow for it."

"You lie! You know you're not going to sell it. You're going to play with it. Know your children hungering for milk and play with the skin!"

"My children!"

"No, God be praised, they're—not—yours," said Groa, allowing the blows to rain on Arni. "But now I'll keep the skin for you." And like an arrow she shot out of the door, all out of breath and trembling.

For a few seconds Arni stood still. His eyes seemed bursting out of their sockets, and the hair in his beard stood on end. In a flash he rushed over the kitchen floor and out of the house.

Groa had just taken the skin down off the nail on the wall. Now she brandished it and looked at Arni with fury in her gaze. But he did not wait. He rushed at her, gave her such a shove that she fell, and, snatching the skin from her, ran. A safe distance away, he turned and stood panting for several seconds. At last, exhausted and trembling with rage, he hissed:

"I tell you, Groa, I'll have my way about this. The skin is the only thing that is all my own, and no one shall take it from me."

Arni fled then. He took to his heels, and ran away as fast as he could up the slopes.

Far in the innermost corner of the outlying sheepcote at Bali, to which the sun's rays never reach, Arni built himself a little cupboard. This cupboard is kept carefully locked, and Arni carries the key on a string which hangs around his neck. Arni now has become quite prosperous. For a long time it was thought that he must keep money in the cupboard, but last spring an acquaintance of his stopped at the outlying sheepcote on his way from the village. The man had some liquor with him and gave Arni a taste. At last the visitor was allowed to see what the cupboard contained—a carefully combed and smoothed dark brown fox skin. Arni was visibly moved by the unveiling of his secret. Staring at the ceiling, he licked his whiskers and sighed deeply.

"It seems to me, Gisli," he said to his friend, "that I'd

rather lose all my ewes than this skin, for it was the thing which once made me say, 'Thus far and no farther!' And since then I seem to own something right here in my breast which not even Jon of Lon can take away from me. I think I am now beginning to understand what is meant in the Scriptures by 'the treasure which neither moth nor rust can corrupt.' "

Arni's red-rimmed eyes were moist. For a while he stood there thinking. But all of a sudden he shook his head and turning to his acquaintance, said: "Let's see the bottle. A man seems to feel warmer inside if he gets a little drop." And Arni shook himself as if the mental strain of his philosophizing had occasioned in him a slight chill.

Kristmann Gudmundsson

THE early years of KRISTMANN GUDMUNDSSON (1902–) were marked by great vicissitudes of fortune, but in the end he emerged victorious over ill health, want, and other trials. While his first literary efforts appeared in Icelandic, his principal works, until the last few years, have been written in Norwegian. Two years after his arrival in Norway he published his first book, *Islandsk Kjaerlighet* (Icelandic Loves, 1926), which not only revealed a remarkable mastery of the Norwegian language, but great narrative talent as well. Since then hardly a year has passed by without a new novel from his hand, and he has won fame in Scandinavia and elsewhere, as his books have been translated into many languages and widely read.

In some of his works, such as the idyl, *Den blaa Kyst* (The Blue Coast, 1931), and in the more mature and substantial story, *Hvite Netter* (White Nights, 1934), the love theme is fundamental. He has, however, achieved even greater literary success with his novels on more general themes, where he deals with life in Iceland, past and present; such as in *Brudekjolen* (*The Bridal Gown*, 1927), his first full-length novel, and *Livets morgen* (*The Morning of Life*, 1929), both of which have been translated into English and published in this country, and *Det hellige Fell* (The Holy Mountain, 1932). Here are revealed his powers of description and characterization, his vivid imagination, not least in recreating the past, and his vigorous and varied style. His novel *Gudinnen og Oksen* (1938), which has appeared in America under the title

Winged Citadel, is a novel on life in the island of Crete about 1500 B. C.

SUCH IS LIFE

TRANSLATED BY MEKKIN SVEINSON PERKINS

JON the Pauper trudged across the homefield with a rope under his arm. He was on his way to the sheepcote to hang himself.

He buttoned his jacket well up around his neck, for it was still early spring; the weather was cold and raw. Dangerous weather, thought he to himself. A man might easily catch pnuemonia unless he took care.

Yes, pneumonia. Jon the Pauper lingered over the word and shuddered. All his life he had feared the disease. His father had died of it; his grandfather also. A man couldn't be too careful, he thought, as he trudged along.

But then he remembered the rope he had under his arm. He smiled slyly and unbuttoned his jacket. Like hell he should be afraid of pneumonia any longer! He would fix that. Wasn't he going to hang himself? What a cheering thought! He was safe from that horrid pneumonia. He was not going to die of pneumonia.

The sheepcote was quite a distance from the homefield. It lay beyond a low sand hill and was not visible from the house. Jon the Pauper reached the bridle path leading down to the village. He walked along slowly. He had all the time in the world. It was Sunday. Everyone was at church. No one to disturb him.

If only a man could get hold of a drop of the good old

brandy to buck him up! It was so good for all kinds of doubts and worries; it steadied a man; made him fearless. But what was the use of thinking about such things now that the world was all crazy, topsy turvy, and aimless? Everything gone to smash; even liquor a thing of the past. Nothing left to gladden a poor old man.

And this last crushing blow—that baby of his, his Thora, that she should be sent to jail—it was more than a man could bear. He had been so happy when she wrote home about the "big man" to whom she was practically engaged. He had also been cheered when he learned that she was expecting a baby. It was fine that his daughter should be having a baby by a "big man" in Reykjavík. The more reason why they should marry. He had looked forward with joy to being grandfather to the child of a "big man" in Reykjavík!

But now she had killed the child and was in the grip of the law. Killed the child of that "big man"! He was even a consul, they said. No, it was too black a disgrace to suffer in his old age. Still, if he could get hold of a drop of brandy as in the days gone by, well maybe! It was long now since he had felt the warmth in his breast, the warmth produced by good strong liquor. His mouth watered.

At the door of the sheepcote he paused and took the snuff horn out of his pocket, blew his nose between his fingers, wiped them off on his pants, and inhaled a large pinch of snuff. Then he sighed with contentment and squinted at the sun. What a godsend snuff was! Almost like the blessed brandy. And men took it into their heads to prohibit a thing like that. Soon they would prohibit snuff.

too. 'Twould be lucky then to be resting under the sod!

Suddenly Jon heard the sound of horses' hoofs on the bridle path. Who in the world could that be? Church could not yet have let out. The dim, old eyes of Jon the Pauper stared. Why, if there wasn't a man on horseback! But how strangely he rode! He was reeling. Now he came closer. Well, if it wasn't the old merchant himself, and riding the bay! Goodness gracious, how unsteadily the man rode! Was he sick? Or drunk? Ah, yes, drunk! A pleasant warmth crept into the breast of Jon the Pauper. Of course, these big men—they had kept a drop or two hidden away when prohibition began. And what a beautiful horse! Oh, if he only had such a horse!

The old merchant was fat and burly and red in the face—a regular "big man." Jon stepped out of the path and retreated to the wall of the sheepcote. He tipped his cap respectfully:

"Good day to you," said he.

"Eh? That you, my dear Jon? Hic!—Whoa, there!—Stand still, damn you, Brunn!" cried the merchant, scolding the nag. "Come here, my dear Jon," he went on, hiccoughing. "I want—hic!—to talk to you." And he held out a fat, hairy hand.

Hurriedly Jon the Pauper wiped his right hand off in his jacket, and he glowed at the merchant's kindly words. "My dear Jon," he had said, and he had even shaken hands. In his whole life no big man had ever shown old Jon the Pauper such honor.

"My dear Jon!"

"Yes, good merchant!" Jon's tone was meek.

"Everything's gone to hell—straight to hell—hic! Everything's all shot. Bankrupt, my dear Jon." There were tears in the merchant's voice.

"What *is* the merchant saying?" asked Jon the Pauper, moving a little closer. It was so sweet, that smell of big men, the smell of good brandy.

"Yes—hic!—broke, ruined. Understand? Everything's gone to the dogs. Have to close up— Lost money—hic! —finished!"

Jon the Pauper let the rope fall. Never in his life had he heard anything so incredible.

"Eh? What do I see? A rope? My dear Jon, if I did as I ought, I'd borrow that and end it all. Understand? Such is life—and I want to tell you, my dear Jon, that life's not worth hanging onto—hic!—not unless you're rich, have money. Understand? But I haven't the courage, my dear Jon; I don't dare hang myself. I've thought it all over—to kill myself either with a razor—or a rope. From now on I don't wish to live, now that everything's gone. You don't know what it is—hic!—to save, to save all your life, a full bank account, big stacks of money, house and goods—be respected—everyone tips his hat—hic!—and to have power, my dear Jon, to have power. And then all at once the war ends. One loss on top of another, and a wretch of a son squandering money out in Copenhagen. Goods don't sell. Lousy farmers don't pay their bills. And then one fine day, bankrupt, broke—hic!—through! That's life! And yet we hang on to it, my dear Jon, with a firm grip—hang on tight."

Jon the Pauper had moved still nearer the merchant.

He stretched out his neck and listened open-mouthed to the great man's words.

But the old merchant straightened in the saddle, and a fierce look came over his face.

"If only that son of Belial hadn't been such a rotten waster! The huge sums I've had to pay out! Then I might perhaps—hic!—have made it. Then I wouldn't be here today, my dear Jon. Ever heard the like? He squanders and strews money about just as if it lay all around like the seaweed on the beach here. You should look at the bills he sends to his poor old father! Gambling debts, suits of clothes, frock coats, bicycles with motors to them, and steaks and fried eggs—hic!—and women, and all kinds of trash. No profits, and the goods I sell are not paid for. And he spends like a prince out there in Copenhagen—like a prince, I say, my dear Jon!"

The merchant stopped for a second and looked reproachfully at Jon.

"Oh, yes—Copenhagen—well, yes—" stammered Jon, retreating a little.

But the merchant's red face now resumed its gentler, more benign expression. "He's been very costly—that boy. But a fine smart kid he is! And the people he meets! But such a darn spendthrift! Well, that's all over now. Now he gets no more. I'm bankrupt, my dear Jon—ruined!"

The old man straightened in the saddle and stared solemnly at Jon the Pauper.

"Ruined!" he quavered with emotion.

"Such is life!" he went on philosophically. "Life is—hic!—no longer worth a rap to me. I'm a fool not to borrow your rope, my dear Jon. But to tell you the truth, I don't dare—don't dare because of the consequences. My son's a lawyer, the young devil! If he'd only get a position and be a help to his old father! Will you—hic!—have a little drink, my dear Jon?"

The old merchant drew a flask out of his pocket. It was half full of liquor. Placing it to his lips, he took a good long draught. Then he handed the flask to Jon.

"There you are, my dear Jon, help yourself. I've always —hic!—liked you. An honest man of the people, content with your station. Not many like that nowadays. No respect for us any more—hic!—your betters, I mean. You are of the good old type, my dear Jon. Help yourself."

Something thawed in the breast of Jon the Pauper; something cold grew warm. He took the flask with trembling hands.

"God bless the merchant!" he muttered. "God bless the merchant!" he repeated. "Always kind to the poor, a good man!" Tears rose in his old eyes as the precious liquor trickled down his throat.

"Don't mention it, my dear Jon," said the merchant, sitting erect on his horse and staring ahead with an injured look in his eyes. "Yes, you are right; I am a good man. But—hic! does anyone take note of that? I may say a philanthropist. Sold at moderate prices. Of course, you understand, a man has to get what's coming to him. But do you think the farmers here understand that? Nothing but arrogance, deceit, and trickery nowadays, my dear Jon. Such is life! If I did the right thing, I'd borrow your rope and end it all. Hic!—All over for me. But the consequences, my dear Jon, I really don't dare!"

Jon the Pauper held out the flask and thanked the merchant.

"God bless you for the liquor, merchant!" The tears ran down his cheeks. "And I'll say this, that if there were many like you—then—yes, then—for you've been a good man and a benefactor to this district. That is my sincere conviction, merchant."

The old merchant had stretched out his hand to receive the flask, but withdrew it when he heard these last words.

"Keep the little that's left, my dear Jon," he said, philanthropically. "It's so good to talk to a humble, an honest man of the people. You understand me so well. We are both old now. Such is life! But I hang on—don't dare—hic!—hang on tight."

The bay had become impatient at the long wait. Now he started off slowly and cautiously, but the old merchant paid no attention to that. "Hang on tight," he said, waving his arms. "Such is life—but—hic!—we hang on tight, my dear Jon."

Jon the Pauper—a stooped and shabby figure of an old man—stood respectfully watching the merchant ride away. In one hand he held the flask; in the other, his cap. He stood thus until the old merchant had disappeared between the hills. Then uttering a sigh as if a load had been lifted from him, he raised the flask against the sun and looked through it.

Even such a big man might have troubles on account of his children, mused Jon. That had not occurred to him before. They had the same sorrow, he and the old merchant. Such was life! The face of Jon the Pauper beamed.

Each had his own burden to bear, he and the old merchant. Yes, indeed! And the smile on his face grew broader still as he dwelt on the fact that the old merchant *did not dare!*

He thrust the flask into his pocket and turned and stared down the path. A warmth crept into his old breast—a happy, a youthful feeling. All his life he had been tormented by the fact that he was so timid and frightened. Now he knew in a flash it took courage to hang yourself. It was known as an act of courage. And the old merchant did not dare.

He pulled the flask out of his pocket and took another swig. To think that he, poor old Jon the Pauper, should be braver than the merchant himself—the old merchant, the big man of the district!

Picking up the rope, he began a leisurely movement in the direction of home, his whole face gradually becoming one big smile. Yes, why in thunder should a man hang himself?

THE CONSCIENCE OF THE SEA

TRANSLATED BY RICHARD BECK

OLD Skipper Hordur was gloomy and silent on the way towards land. Although the sea was smooth as a mirror, he stood at the helm of the fishing-boat himself.

The sun was shining, and the weather was warm. Most of the crew were sleeping in the forecastle. Only a few were sitting on the hatch, smoking. All were tired and lazy after the storm and the toil. Probably there would not be long rest for them either, now during the busiest herring season, if they knew old Hordur right!

The two men on the hatch chatted softly while they stole a glance toward the man at the wheel. It was strange indeed how sullen the old man was today, when all had gone so well. He did not seem to look forward to reaching land with a full boat, and without having lost so much as one foot of his net in that driving squall they got into yesterday evening. Surely, not everyone had escaped so luckily from that episode.

But it was wisest not to ask any questions when old Hordur was in this mood. He was subject to such fits, the crosspatch. And besides one can forgive an old weather-beaten seaman much—when he has fisherman's luck and is reasonable towards his crew. A seaman like Hordur was not to be found everywhere, and one would have to seek far for the equal of his luck in fishing.

Skipper Hordur stared intently towards land. In there, between the two purple hills to the south, lay Knaravik, his home.

If only no misfortune had occurred there at home! He had not had a moment's peace since they escaped so fortunately from the storm yesterday. Just think that not even a hawser or a piece of net had been lost! Such a thing was truly aggravating. He had in fact delayed hauling in the net in order to give the sea plenty of time. If the net had only been ripped so that they had lost a little of all the herring, then he could have been at ease now. But no! The net and the herring were safe on board, and the boat was so heavily loaded that it moved with difficulty through the water.

Continued good luck all summer long! Bless me, if that did not make one uneasy. And not a single accident all last summer either!

Old Hordur snatched his snuff-box and took a generous pinch. He became more and more ominously gloomy. What was the matter now with the motor? Could not that rascal of a boy get it to work properly? The boat hardly moved from the spot!

"Gvendur!"

"Yes, what is it, skipper?"

"Can't you oil the motor properly, boy!"

"Ye-es. I have oiled it all right," came sleepily from the engine-room.

Hordur cleared his throat sharply and spat.

The sea lay clear and calm to the east and the west and the north, lay as if in wait for something, so it seemed to old Hordur. He looked at it with angry eyes and cursed a little. It was never to be trusted, and least of all when it lay so smooth and calm.

No, one could never feel safe with the sea. From him whom it gave most it also took most. True enough, there was a kind of justice in all that it did, nevertheless. Had the net only been torn yesterday! It would have been a loss of several hundred kroner, and one could have got by with that for no end of time. Regardless of how many faults one could find with the sea, it did have a conscience. He had experienced that many a time.

One had to admit that it repaid what it took—in its own way.

For instance, once during a stormy night his best motor-boat was torn from its moorings and smashed on the

Knararvik beach; the following spring he had to go into big debt to buy a new one. But then there came three exceptionally good years in succession so that he could pay for the boat and more.

Yes, the sea did have a conscience. It gave one much, and was often generous; and then there was really a certain fairness in its demanding some offerings in return for what it gave.

He always made good catches after an accident. But he had never seen so much herring and fish in the sea as the year after his son was drowned.

Ah, yes, it was sad to recall. He was only fourteen, the youngster, and all his heart was set on the sea. He had just got a new small skiff, and he used to sail it on the creek and outside, when there was a good wind.

Hordur himself was at sea when the accident happened. It was a bright morning just like this, but a fresh wind blew from the east. He was returning from a trip with the boat full of herring. He had had good luck for a long time. When he brought the boat alongside the wharf, they came carrying the corpse.

But that time it also seemed as if the sea itself felt that it had taken too great a toll. Throughout that summer and the next as well, he had incredibly good luck. He filled the boat with fish almost every time, even if the others did not catch a thing. It was for him a year of success in every way; and at last he had almost forgiven the sea. After all, one did not get anything for nothing in this world.

All that he possessed he owed to the sea, and it was good to own a little. For his part he did not need a great deal;

but it was the boy he had left. He had such a passion for books and studies and the like. He was to graduate from college, as they called it, next spring. Now he was at home on his holidays.

The boy! Skipper Hordur gave a start at the thought. Obviously what had happened had to do with the boy. For something had happened. He felt that so clearly. What if the boy had taken the skiff and started sailing it and—capsized! Just that had happened to the oldest boy. And then, just as now, he had felt that something had happened.

"Gvendur!"

"Yes—what is it, skipper!"

"Oil the motor, confound it!"

If the sea had taken the boy from him, it might just as well take everything, including himself! Old Hordur scowled grimly out over the shining, friendly sea.

How well he remembered the old days when the little fellow met him on the beach. He always jumped up into his arms, pulled him by the beard, and used him for a riding-horse. And how he laughed and shrieked for joy! Skipper Hordur could not help grinning broadly when he came to think about it.

There were crowds of people down on the beach when old Hordur turned into the creek. The old man stood at the helm himself. The crew had huddled together forward.

Skipper Hordur looked neither to the right nor to the left. Nor up towards the beach. He stared straight ahead and steered in the direction of his large storehouse yonder.

All the time he kept an eye on his home up on the mountainside. It was so quiet up there. But down on the beach crowds of people were standing. He saw that well

enough, and it could bode no good. They should not have the satisfaction of seeing sorrow or tears on the part of old Skipper Hordur! He would at least be man enough for that.

Now they would soon reach land.

But—but what in the world was the matter with the wharf! Hordur did not see it until now. The wharf was gone. Only a few poles were left standing.

He did not take time to ponder over it, for from the house above a young man came running down to the beach. Old Hordur's face lit up. Surely there was the dear boy, his own living self, after all!

The young man stood grave and downcast at the water mark when Hordur jumped ashore.

"The wharf, father," he said. "We couldn't do anything to save it."

Skipper Hordur grinned broadly. Then, with his large seaman's fists, he seized the young man by the shoulders and shook him.

"The wharf, you say, my boy? What the devil do we care about the rotten planks! But listen now. Go and see if you can't find some bottles of good old brandy out in the stable-loft. When we have unloaded the boat we'll slip up there and have a taste!"

The crew suddenly got busy. The brown, weather-beaten faces were bright with smiles, and winked at each other. Didn't I say so? Old Hordur was always like that. Impossible to figure that fellow out.

But Skipper Hordur stood broad and smiling on the beach. He fetched out his snuff-box, tapped the lid, and took a pinch. Then he gazed around thoughtfully and caught sight of the skiff which lay undamaged high on the beach.

"You might as well have taken that, too," he mumbled with a confidential nod to the sea, which lay out there and slumbered in the sun. Then he coughed and grinned. "But I must say that this time you were not so unreasonable at that!"

Halldór Kiljan Laxness

HALLDÓR KILJAN LAXNESS (1902–   ) is the globe-trotter among present-day Icelandic authors and the stormy petrel in their midst as well. His varied production in the form of essays, poems, short stories, and novels, ranges over a vast field. Foreign influences and strong native impulses blend in his works, which have often in a fundamental manner broken with the accepted literary tradition, and hence been the cause of much controversy. His radical political views—he is far to the left in such matters—have naturally fanned the flames of the opposition to him, although he has always had equally fervent admirers and champions. Such are the extremes in his literary art and style that a leading Icelandic critic has compared them with the many-sided tonal blending of a symphony orchestra.

Typical of the mature work of Laxness, although in some respects surpassed by his later novels, all of which are largely broad social satires of Icelandic life in town and country, is his two-volume serial *Salka Valka* (1931–1932), which appeared in English translation in 1936. Written in colorful and eloquent style, this and his other works, although frequently marred by excesses, are obviously the product of an author endowed with keen observation, strong power of characterization, and remarkable narrative talent. Unquestionably, he is the most gifted of the younger Icelandic novelists. His great mastery of language, psychological penetration, and rare story-telling ability are strikingly revealed in his latest novel, the last part of a major four-volume series, rich in poetic beauty in spite of the fact that it is the story of untold human suffering and not a little sordidness. Laxness has had great influence on a number of contemporary Icelandic writers.

LILY

The Story of Nebuchadnezzar Nebuchadnezzarson in Life and in Death

TRANSLATED BY AXEL EYBERG AND JOHN WATKINS

I GAVE the man this name just so that people would take notice of the story and think to themselves: "Ah, this must be an amusing story!" Otherwise I might have let it suffice to call him N. N., although neither of these names was used at the funeral which was held in connection with his demise. The truth is that I have either forgotten what his name was or have never really known it for certain. But what does that matter? For as you notice there is another name above that one, and this first name is really much more important, as we shall see when we have finished the story.

It is really a very long story. Indeed, it is so tremendously long that when I start thinking about it, I am often shocked at how long it is. . . . And yet it began with one of the shortest melodies I have ever heard. In fact it could hardly be called a melody. It was rather a fragment of a melody, the latter half of a short melody, and the biggest part of it was a single concluding note. And that one note was so long drawn out that from any consideration of reasonable proportion, one could rightly have imagined it to be the end of a great symphony by one of the better known composers. Thus with the higher art in mind I have passed this fragment of melody on to an acquaintance of mine who aspires to become a composer, so that he may use it in a symphony when he has attained sufficient stature and when the world has begun to take an interest in those melodies which have their origin in the respiratory organs of the people of Snæfellsnes.

Now we shall hear the story.

It was when I was a student and lived in a basement in Reykjavík, in a wretched little hole separated only by a thin partition from the furnace room. One winter I noticed that this melody was always being sung, especially late in the evening after the fire had been banked for the night, in a dull hoarse voice like a wavy and woolly line. And on the last note it was as though the singer had forgotten to take a breath, so that finally the note died out and silence came of itself, as if the singer had died like the tone. Time passed, and nothing more was heard from him. But in a little while a kind of mumbling became audible, and this mumbling struggled hard to become musical notes, with long pauses in between, and it was obvious that the melody continued to live in the singer's breast, although the voice was hoarse and cracked and the tones came to grief on the vocal chords. Yet it never happened that the singer did not ultimately find himself again in this short melody with that long note, which, as has been mentioned before, is destined to become a great symphony.

Thus did he sing for me in the stillness, night after night, as the winter passed, and when I began to investigate the source of this evening song, I discovered that it was the man who looked after the furnace. As midnight approached, he went away.

One evening I went into the little nook where the furnace stood. The embers glowed red in the darkness behind the half-open furnace door. And in front of the furnace sat Nebuchadnezzar Nebuchadnezzarson, almost invisible in the darkness, and sang.

"Good-evening," said I.

"Good-evening," came the answer from the darkness in an old, hoarse voice.

"It's warm here," said I.

"I'm leaving," said he.

"Isn't this your room?" I asked.

"No," said he.

"Oh, isn't it?" said I. "But still I've often heard you singing here in the evenings."

"I'm leaving," he said apologetically and got up.

"Oh, please don't go on my account. I just dropped in to see you because I've so often heard you sing."

"I don't sing," said he.

"But I've often heard you," I protested.

"No," said he. "I've never been able to sing."

"I've learned the melody," I said.

But he merely muttered something to himself and tried to slip out through the door behind me.

"Don't let me disturb you," I said.

"It's bedtime," he said and left.

One time in frost and snow I was shown a piano case behind some privies down by the shore. There lived Nebuchadnezzar Nebuchadnezzarson. Perhaps the man gets his inclination for music from living in a piano box, I thought.

A few evenings passed in silence.

But as time went on he forgot me again and began to

sing as before the same fragment of melody with the same long note that died away. Then I went in to him again.

"Good-evening," said I.

"Good-evening," said he.

"You're singing," said I.

"No," said he.

"Where did you learn this melody?" I asked.

"Melody? That's no melody."

"But you're always singing one tune."

"I don't sing," he said. "I've never been able to sing."

"You hum," I protested.

Then he said: "I used to long to be able to sing at one time. But that's past. I never even think of it now. I just sit here in front of the furnace sometimes when I have finished banking the fire. But now I'm leaving."

"Where are you from?" I asked.

"From the West," he answered.

"Where in the West?"

"From Olafsvik."

"Is that a good place?"

"The sea is rough at Olafsvik as elsewhere," said he.

"Have you relations in the West?"

"They're dead."

"What did you do in the West?"

"What did I do? I did whatever came along, sometimes on sea, sometimes on land. All depending on what came along."

"Why did you come to Reykjavík?"

He was silent for a long time and finally replied: "It's all up with the West long ago. It's all up with the West."

"You were doubtless right in coming to Reykjavík," I

said. "In my opinion Reykjavík is a much more agreeable place to live than anywhere else in the country."

He was silent for a long time and sat there on a box in front of the furnace. This time there was a light in the little furnace room, so he looked straight down at the holes in the toes of his boots.

"My first night here I slept in the cemetery," he said.

"Did you really?" I exclaimed, and added in order to cheer him up: "There are many who have had to be content to sleep more than one night in the cemetery."

"Yes," said he.

His cheeks were grimy and he had a gray beard that did not look as if it had been brushed.

"Your shoes are in bad shape," said I.

"That doesn't bother me," said he. "I found them down at Vatnsmyri the year before last. Somebody must have forgotten them in the peat bog."

He stood up and took down his hat, which was hanging on a nail behind the furnace. It was one of those derbies which business men wear when they are new, but which are generally thrown into the ash can when a rent appears between the crown and the brim or when some child has stuck a knife through the top.

"May I see your hat?" I said.

The hole in the top was big enough for a child's fist.

"Your hat's getting pretty old," I said, looking up at the ceiling through the hole. "But it has obviously been a good hat in its day."

I handed him back his hat. He took it and he too looked through the hole.

"It's not everybody that can read the Lord's Prayer

through his hat," said he with a grimace. He had only one tooth.

Then the blessed spring came. It is never so tempting to loll out of the window and look at precisely everything that goes on in the street, especially the most trivial things, as in the spring when one is studying for examinations. At such a time one reads into what goes on in the street various learned significances.

On moving day a new family moved into one of the apartments on the middle floor of the house. I had somehow or other become aware of it, but of course it was no concern of mine. It was a man and his wife. They had one daughter, she might have been eight years old. Her name was Lily, and I guessed from her appearance that the couple were out-of-town people, for she had braids, they were blonde braids, and she wore homemade woollen stockings. The little girl played with the other children in the yard outside my window, and her mother was terribly fond of her, for she leaned out of her window on the second floor most of the day directing the girl like a regiment with resolute commands:

"Look out for the car! Look out for the drunk man! Look out for the dog! Lily! Lily! Look out for the police!"

This was at the time when there were still old stone fences built of ordinary field stones between the lots in the town, and on the other side of the street there was one of these fences with a little green field behind it. But this was a rather quiet street, and on the fence sat Nebuchadnezzar Nebuchadnezzarson in the blue spring sunshine watching the children play in the yard. Admiration shone from the grimy face, through the unkempt beard. But as the day passed, the children grew tired and went home for a bite to eat. Lily was left alone in the yard playing hop-scotch all by herself, and then Nebuchadnezzar Nebuchadnezzarson called:

"Lily."

But she pretended not to hear and kept on hopping on one foot as if she were extremely interested in winning the game, and then Nebuchadnezzar Nebuchadnezzarson called again:

"Lily, my dear!"

But she still pretended not to hear and only after a little while did she look up at the window to see whether her mother was still there, but her mother had gone out into the kitchen to cook.

"Hasn't little Lily got anything to say to the old fellow Nebuchadnezzar Nebuchadnezzarson today?" he asked, from the fence. And he drew up out of his pocket a little paper bag which he had kept hidden all this time. At this the little girl walked straight across the street, a bit skeptically, with her hands behind her back, and looked down into his paper bag. Then she looked up at the window. There were raisins, if you please, in the bag. She still acted as if she were not surprised at this and had little or no interest in it. But it wound up with their both sitting on the fence munching raisins, she ten to his one. At first she dangled her legs shyly and looked critically at his unkempt beard. Then she went on playing hop-scotch on the street in front of him. Her mother called down from the window and told her to come in to supper, but she came back in a little while because she knew there was still something left in the bag.

Thus the spring passed, and before long Lily was no longer skeptical of Nebuchadnezzar Nebuchadnezzarson, but ran to meet him when she saw him coming, dived into his pocket, and found for herself the bag of raisins. And sometimes in the evening they sat for a long time on the fence, and I felt sure the old man was telling the little girl stories, because she listened so attentively to what he was saying.

"Are they some relation to you, these people?" I asked, meaning the little girl's parents.

"They're from the West," he said.

"Then you know something about them?"

"Yes," said he. "That's her—Lily."

I couldn't quite make the man out. He seemed to me rather strange, but I didn't bother about that. It was no concern of mine. I had other things to think about. And even if I had discovered that these people were not from the West at all, but from the East, I shouldn't have felt like arguing about it with the old fellow.

He was just about twenty, I heard him say, and they had always known each other. She was just a few months younger. He offered to build her a little house on the Snout, with a tiny lawn and a vegetable patch, as was then the custom. At that time he was fishing on shares with the late Gudmundur, skipper of the *Hope*, and was doing well. But he never could sing. Her name was Lily.

"And then what?" asked the little girl.

But I had no time to eavesdrop any longer and thought to myself: "He's just telling her some old story from the West."

In the autumn, I came back from the North, and one

day as I was chatting with some friends on the street corner, I noticed a man standing staring at me a short distance away. He waited for me to say goodbye to them, and when I had done so, he overtook me and stretched out his dirty hand: "Nebuchadnezzar Nebuchadnezzarson."

"What's new?" I asked.

"Nothing," he answered.

"Was there something you wanted?"

"No," said he. "I just wanted to see whether you'd recognize me."

"Of course," I said. "And what's more, I still know our melody. How's your little girl friend?"

"They've taken away my old-age pension," he said, "—that thirty crowns."

"Why?"

"That fellow Joseph said I was using it to buy raisins. But you must know a lot about the law."

"Who is that fellow Joseph?"

"He's a relation of mine. He sometimes helps me out with a little fish or something."

"Look here," I said, "you ought to go to the mayor about that." For I didn't have time.

"I don't know," said he. "It doesn't make much difference. I may perhaps be able to get a house this winter."

"A house?"

"Yes, like last year."

"Aren't you going to look after the furnace in the house you had last year any more?"

"No," said he. "It's all up with everything in that house. It's all up with that house."

"How's that?"

"Oh, I dunno," he said.

"Goodbye," said I.

"Goodbye, sir," said he. "And thanks for your kindness."

He lifted his hat.

I did not see him again to take any notice of him until many years later. I was then a medical student. He was carried into the morgue in a sheet, and I recognized him although he had been cleaned up. I had no feeling for him beyond that which one has for dead men who have been outcasts of society, and it was not until after the funeral held in connection with his demise that I noticed the congruity in his life and death. This was a man of whom nobody expected anything. He was found dead in his piano box. Nobody really knew his name or where he came from, much less what had been the aim of his life. Even on this dissection day I could not remember the melody he had sung. One thing was certain: he was carved up with scientific precision, and we scrutinized his insides with more attention than he had ever been looked at from the outside in all his life.

But why should I be telling about this here? It is long since I lost interest in medical science and turned to other subjects. But as so many years have gone by since then, I shall confess that a little fraud was practised upon him in the name of science. As a matter of fact, his bones were removed and polished. His skeleton is now used for scientific observation—I shall not say where—but the rest of the corpse was discarded. This was a scientific secret and conspiracy, and we put gravel in the coffin. One of the group took charge of that, and we followed him to the grave, a few of us medical students, in order to prevent anybody from taking a peek at the corpse at the last moment. We carried the coffin into the church and out again.

It was indeed a day of appalling irony. It was just two days before Christmas. The funeral was rushed through before it was quite daylight, and what made it extraordinary was the circumstance that the church was draped in black ceremonial crepe, because at noon on this very same day was to be buried one of the most distinguished consuls-general in the city. As has been said, Nebuchadnezzar Nebuchadnezzarson was squeezed in on account of the effrontery of the cemetery officials, who proclaimed that, because of the Christmas celebrations so near at hand, this man would have to be buried today or never. And it was a downright scandal that such a no-account funeral should be held with the church hung in mourning.

A northeaster was blowing and we hustled the coffin in through a shower of hail. Our chief worry was that the bottom might fall out and the gravel spill down on the church floor in the midst of all this solemnity and sorrow. And when we got half way up the aisle I became so agitated by the creaking of the shoddy coffin that I could not keep my tongue off the silly fool who had been charged with "laying out" the gravel. Besides, the weight of the coffin was well nigh crushing us. We sat down in the front pew as if we were some sort of relations of the deceased, and the pastor hurried in from the vestry looking rather shamefaced, as was to be expected, over this misuse of the mourning draperies (God help us if the Consul's family should get word of it!), and delivered like a shot the brief funeral sermon he had held the week before over an insignificant woman from out of town. Naturally he tripped up time and again when he was supposed to say "our late beloved brother" and it was written in the sermon "our beloved sister." Once he even blurted out that "this late beloved sister of ours was sorely lamented by her surviving husband and children in another part of the country." I was deathly afraid that somebody would notice this nonsense and looked back over my shoulder into the church. But the funeral procession, aside from the undertaker, consisted solely of one old woman, deaf I hoped, who sat far back in the church, and I tried to console myself with the idea that she had come in only to get out of the hail and had otherwise no interest in who was being buried.

But when we had carried the coffin out again and the hearse had begun to crawl away, who should make as if to follow to the cemetery but this old woman with her black Sunday shawl around her wrinkled face and her blue striped apron? So I and two others saw nothing else for it but to trudge along behind to keep an eye on things and if necessary to prevent the old woman from raising a rumpus at the cemetery. For indeed we could not feel easy about this funeral until the grave had been filled in. Finally, however, my two companions wearied of this wandering, and slipped off into the Café Uppsala, and it fell upon me to keep watch on the funeral procession all the way. So we tramped along after the coffin, this old woman and I, with the pastor and the undertaker, both in high silk hats.

After the grave had been filled in and the pastor and the undertaker had gone, the old woman stood there still, looking at the earth in the hail storm. I lingered at the gate of the cemetery, but she did not come, so I turned back to the grave again.

"What are you waiting for anyway, my good woman?" I asked. "Did you know this man?"

She looked at me half in fear, and when she finally tried to answer, her face contorted with pain, her lips trembled, and the corners of her mouth dropped, so that I could see she had lost her teeth. And her old red eyes filled with tears. I have described somewhere before how unpleasant it is to see old people cry.

"Don't cry, my good woman," I said. "He is with God."

"Yes," she said and dried her tears with the corner of her apron.

"You ought to go home before you get a chill," said I, for I did not want the woman to hang around there any longer.

We walked together through the cemetery.

"Who are you?" I asked.

"I come from the West," she said.

"You are not from Olafsvik?"

"Yes."

"Then you knew him of course."

"Yes, we were of the same age. Then I married in the South. I lived for forty years in Keflavik."

"What is your name?"

"My name is Lily."

"Is your husband living?"

"No, he died long ago."

"Have you any children?"

"Oh, I've brought thirteen of them into the world,"

answered the woman with such a resigned note in her voice that I understood at once that she must have at least sixty grandchildren.

"There are many strange things," I said. "He was always lonely."

She trudged along silently at my side over the grave mounds and I hardly expected that she would answer me further; a new storm was on its way across Skerjafjörd. So I prepared to take leave of her in the gate of the cemetery and took off my hat.

"Goodbye," I said.

She stretched out to me her old, bony hand and looking straight at me, the only partaker in her grief, she said: "I too was always lonely."

And then her face again got out of control and again she raised the corner of her apron to her eyes and turned away.

And here ends the story of Nebuchadnezzar Nebuchadnezzarson, who spent only one night in the cemetery.